Data Privacy Across Borders

Crafting Corporate Strategies

Lambert Hogenhout

Amanda Wang

Technics Publications

Published by:

115 Linda Vista, Sedona, AZ 86336 USA
https://www.TechnicsPub.com

Edited by Sadie Hoberman
Cover design by Lorena Molinari

First Printing 2023
Copyright © 2023 by Lambert Hogenhout and Amanda Wang

ISBN, print ed.	9781634623926
ISBN, Kindle ed.	9781634623933
ISBN, ePub ed.	9781634623940
ISBN, PDF ed.	9781634623957

Library of Congress Control Number: 2023948717

Contents

Introduction

In May 2023, Facebook owner Meta was fined €1.2 billion ($1.3B). Two years earlier, Amazon had been fined €746 million. We hear news about data privacy infringements every month, including concerns about mobile apps and Artificial Intelligence (AI) platforms. It is clear that data privacy is becoming an important issue for businesses that use data across borders – and in our rapidly digitizing world, that will soon mean almost all businesses.

It is not just about potential fines. Most businesses depend on the trust of their customers and partners, and handling data responsibly is key to maintaining that trust. A data scandal can damage a company's reputation and market share, whereas transparency and diligence can enhance how the public views a brand. Some companies have started using their data privacy commitments as a strategic differentiator.

This book provides a guide to formulating an approach to Data Privacy (DP) for multinational organizations. In today's environment, where massive amounts of personal data are being collected, processed, and shared, organizations face increasing scrutiny and legal obligations to protect individuals' privacy rights. While there are resources tailored to specific jurisdictions, many organizations handle data that is collected globally. The implications of that in terms of compliance, but also in terms of maintaining the trust of your clients, partners, or stakeholders around the world, can become very complex. To add to the complexity, various online platforms for mobile apps (iOS and Android) and social networks have their own requirements for data privacy. So, if your organization uses these as part of their products or services, or in their engagement with customers, you must also comply with their terms of service.

The challenge is growing weekly as personal data plays a role in more systems. Imagine your car keeps track of your location over time. Now, suppose that a crime happened somewhere around that time. Then, the data collected about you is *highly personal* in the sense that it may provide you an alibi (or make you a suspect!). The European GDPR, among others, recognizes such data specifically and requires you to treat it with extra care. It is important to note that there are benefits to having location data in your car. GPS vehicle tracking systems are helpful in scenarios where if your car is stolen or gets towed, it could aid in recovering it, or in case of an accident, it can help emergency responders locate you quicker. It is also useful in protecting loved ones, such as monitoring a teenager's driving or an elder parent's activities. There has to be a balance between utility (services or products provided to customers) and respect for their rights (data privacy and protection).

The book aims to clarify the main privacy regulations worldwide, explain the challenges in operating with data in a multinational organization, and provide concrete advice on formulating a corporate strategy for data privacy that achieves compliance and risk management and builds trust, internally and externally. Indeed, it is a practical guide to planning such a strategy. The strategy will include a data privacy *program* – specific instructions on how data is being protected and data privacy respected in various business processes as well as broader aspects of corporate strategy and culture.

We wrote this book for Data Privacy Officers, Chief Data Officers, Chief Information Officers, Legal Officers, and other executives in international firms, data practitioners, small business owners, application developers, and anyone else dealing with data in a multinational context. It assumes a basic understanding of data privacy and protection. While the first two chapters introduce the topic, this part is brief. If you need a more thorough introduction to data privacy, refer to the Resources section.

This book is not legal advice. While it can help you understand the process of formulating a strategy and help you get started, the details about various regulations are for informational purposes only and are very much simplified (most of the regulations would merit a whole book in themselves, and these books exist). In fact, the phrasing of certain aspects of regulations and topics here is imprecise from a legal perspective. In most cases, there are legal definitions that define in more detail what is meant, what is allowed, or what is covered. We aim to keep the book readable for a wide audience and explain the general concepts from a strategic perspective. This is why we use plain language (as opposed to "legalese"), where we can and intentionally omit certain aspects of regulations. Of course, once you start implementing your data privacy strategy, you will want to study the details and precise legal definitions and/or get help from a legal professional.

This book does not offer a turnkey solution for your organization nor delve into the details of a privacy program implementation. It offers an understanding of the problem space and a methodology to tackle this space. Working out the details of your strategy and, eventually, your program, as well as implementing it, will take time. In larger organizations, it should be done in collaboration with the IT department, the data management team, and the legal team.

Each of the seven chapters in this book focuses on a specific aspect of data privacy regulations, challenges, and strategies, providing detailed information, practical examples, and actionable guidance:

- **Chapter 1: The Fundamentals of Data Privacy Regulations**. Explores the historical context that led to the development of these regulations, including notorious breaches and other scandals. The chapter introduces key concepts and terminology related to data privacy, such as personal information, consent, legitimate interest, data controllers, and data processors. Also, we cover the motivations behind data privacy regulations, emphasizing the need to balance innovation and technological advancements with individuals' right to privacy. It explores the ethical and societal considerations surrounding data collection and processing practices, laying the foundation for understanding the regulatory landscape. An experienced data privacy practitioner can skip this chapter.

- **Chapter 2: Understanding Personal Data and the Principles for Protection**. Focuses on understanding personal data and the various categories of information within its scope. We also review the principles and best practices for protecting personal data, discussing the concept of data minimization, purpose limitation, and storage limitations. An experienced data privacy practitioner can skip this chapter.

- **Chapter 3: The Global Landscape of Data Privacy Regulations.** Shares a number of examples of regulations from various regions and countries: The European Union, The United States, Canada, China, Singapore, India, South Africa, and Brazil. The idea is to give you a flavor of the various kinds of regulations you may encounter. This knowledge will serve as a foundation for later chapters, where we learn to design an organizational strategy.

- **Chapter 4: The Challenges of Data Privacy in Multinational Operations.** Raises the challenges faced by organizations operating globally in terms of reconciling disparate data privacy regulations. It starts by emphasizing the importance of understanding the multinational character of the operations of one's organization from the perspective of data flows. The Chapter then explores the challenges of the conflicting regulations and cross-border data flows. Chapter 4 also discusses cultural and ethical considerations and the need to balance privacy rights with business objectives in different cultures—building trust and transparency in diverse cultural environments.

- **Chapter 5: Creating a Strategy for Data Privacy in Multinational Organizations.** Shows you how to design a strategy for DP for a global organization.

The Chapter explores the essential ingredients in a corporate approach to data privacy that can satisfy compliance requirements in multiple countries and maintain sensitivity to multiple cultures and groups of stakeholders. It presents a methodology composed of concrete steps to design such a strategy. It discusses strategies such as implementing a global privacy framework based on common principles or adopting a risk-based approach to prioritize compliance efforts. Chapter 5 also discusses the interplay between a data privacy strategy and the organization's data strategy, IT strategy, and risk management framework. By the end of Chapter 5, readers will have learned a methodology to design a data privacy strategy that will work in small or large organizations.

- **Chapter 6: Further Considerations in Implementation.** Although implementation is beyond the scope of this book, a high-level implementation plan may be part of or accompany the strategy. We explore a few specific elements of such an implementation plan, including the role and responsibilities of the Data Protection Officer (DPO), Data Privacy Impact Assessments (DPIAs), Consent Management, Data Breach Notification, and Incident Response.

- **Chapter 7: Future trends in Global Data Privacy.** Data Privacy is a field evolving continuously, and not in the least because of technological developments. New technologies such as AI present new data privacy concerns. At the same time, new technologies are also being invented to support data privacy. We explore the future challenges and considerations of data privacy and data protection. It focuses on emerging technologies such as Artificial Intelligence (including Generative AI platforms like OpenAI's GPT family of products) and their impact on data privacy and protection. It also discusses Privacy Enhancing Technologies (PETs) such as Homomorphic Encryption, Zero-knowledge Proofs, and Multi-party Computation, which are just at the point where they are starting to be used in practice. We also cover the privacy implications of the Metaverse and virtual environments in general.

CHAPTER 1

About Data Privacy Regulations

D ata privacy regulations represent an evolution of legal and societal norms in response to the proliferation of technology in our everyday lives. To comprehend the basis of these regulations, we must delve into the historical context leading to their development, appreciate the impact of notable privacy breaches, and understand the public outcry and demands for more stringent measures to protect personal data. Next, we will learn some key concepts and terminology in data privacy. Finally, we will take a peek into the future, as the field of data privacy is rapidly evolving.

Historical context

The idea of government privacy regulations was driven by evolving technology and growing societal concerns about the Digital Revolution. With the invention of computers and the Internet, the amount of data collected, processed, and stored by individuals, companies, and governments increased exponentially. Data became a key asset for companies in sectors like advertising, marketing, and technology. These companies often collected and used personal data in ways that were not fully transparent to users. Numerous high-profile cases of data breaches and misuse, in which personal data was leaked or used without consent, have drawn public attention to data privacy issues. And it is not only profit-driven companies that are guilty here. In numerous countries, widespread governmental and corporate surveillance, often justified by national security or business interests, have sparked public debate about the balance between security and privacy.

The 2013 revelations of Edward Snowden, a former US National Security Agency (NSA) contractor, were a critical turning point. Snowden disclosed numerous global surveillance programs, many run by the NSA and the Five Eyes Intelligence Alliance, stirring an international debate about privacy, surveillance, and the balance between national security and individual rights.

Over time, these events have pressured governments to take action and enact regulations to protect personal data.

In the private sector, the repercussions of poor data management have been felt globally. For instance, the 2017 Equifax data breach exposed the personal data of approximately 147 million people in the United States, including their Social Security Numbers and addresses. This breach highlighted the vast amount of personal data corporations hold and the risks associated with inadequate security measures. Facebook's Cambridge Analytica scandal in 2018 was another significant wake-up call. The political consulting firm harvested the personal data of millions of Facebook users without their consent for political advertising purposes. This event ignited a broader conversation about consent, the use of personal data for micro-targeting, and the influence of digital platforms on democratic processes.

The sudden popularity of ChatGPT in 2023 also raised questions about data privacy. Especially since this new brand of Generative AI was notoriously un-explainable and un-transparent. It has been trained on terabytes of public data, some of which is personal. It has also been trained on copyrighted writings and artworks, some of which it uses to generate new content. The legalities of this are still being discussed.

As technology keeps evolving, machines and algorithms can glance the tiniest details out of pools and streams of data that were considered relatively safe in the past because of their sheer size. The Internet has also made it easier for data to be collected and shared across borders. Social networks, music streaming, and email services in the cloud have made it even harder to trace where your information is traveling. Countries have differing standards for data privacy, leading to concerns about data being transferred to countries with lower privacy standards. This has been a significant factor in pushing for global standards and regulations on data privacy.

Over the years, the understanding of privacy as a human right has evolved, with the United Nations declaring privacy an integral part of human dignity and personal autonomy. This ethical consideration has been a major driving force for many data privacy regulations.

Key concepts and terminology

These categories of basic concepts and principles are frequently used by data privacy regulations:

- Basic definitions (personal data, data processor and data controller, special categories of data, group privacy)

- Principles for data collection (purpose, consent, data minimization, public interest, legitimate interest)

- Principles for data ownership (accountability, accuracy, risk, storage limitation, disposal)

- The scope of regulations (material scope, territorial scope)

- Concepts related to the rights of citizens (data portability, being informed, access, rectification, objection, erasure)

Personal data

At the heart of data privacy lies *personal data*. This refers to any information that can be used to identify an individual. This can include names, addresses, IP addresses, and more. A more specific term that is often used in regulations and policies is Personally Identifiable Information (PII). PII refers to any information that can be used on its own or with other data to identify, contact, or locate a single person, or to identify an individual in context. Examples include names, Social Security Numbers, email addresses, bank account details, and even digital fingerprints like IP addresses or cookie IDs.

We won't go into more detail here as the next chapter will explore the topic of personal data.

Data subject

The most important role in data privacy regulations is the *Data Subject*. This is an identified or identifiable natural person to whom specific personal data pertains. An identifiable natural person, or data subject, is one who can be identified, directly or indirectly, particularly by reference to an identifier such as a name, an identification number, location data, an online identifier, or to one or more factors specific to the physical, physiological, genetic, mental, economic, cultural, or social identity of that natural person. For example, if a company collects data such as name, email, location, or IP address from users of its website, those users are the data subjects. As data subjects, they have certain rights under data protection laws.

Data processor and data controller

Two other significant roles can be defined in the handling of data: the *data controller* and the *data processor*. The data controller is the entity that determines the purposes and means of processing personal data. In contrast, the data processor is the party that processes data on behalf of the controller. Both roles come with distinct responsibilities and obligations under various data privacy regulations. For example, suppose Anna has set up a home business making jewelry and sells her work online on a website. She uses the logistics company SwiftParcel to deliver the orders. She collects her customers' names and addresses and provides these to SwiftParcel. Here, Anna is the data controller – she determines why and how personal data is processed. SwiftParcel is the data processor – they process personal data on Anna's behalf and follow her instructions.

Purpose

In the context of data privacy, the term *purpose* refers to the specific reason or rationale for collecting, processing, storing, and using personal data. This is important because it often determines whether the collection of data is fair or legal under particular legislations. Generally, the way *purpose* is stated must be explicit, legitimate, and necessary. Often, the *purpose* must be shared with Data Subjects when obtaining their consent.

Of course, is would not be fair to change your mind afterward and use the data for different purposes. Therefore, many regulations include the concept of a *purpose limitation*, which says that data should not be collected or processed in ways incompatible with the stated purpose.

Consent

This means the agreement from the data subject to have their data collected, stored, processed, shared, or otherwise handled. In many cases, personal data can only be processed if the data subject has given consent. Many regulations define consent in specific ways – not any type of clicking of a button or signature on a form will do. Generally, consent must be freely given, specific, informed, and unambiguous.

Data breach

A data breach is a security incident in which unauthorized individuals gain access to, alter, disclose, or destroy personal data. Regulations often have specific requirements from data controllers or processors for procedures to follow when a breach is detected – typically involving notification of the data subjects and/or regulatory authorities.

Territorial scope

This means the geographical area where the law applies. This may be the territory of the country in question but may well extend further (known as extraterritorial reach). For instance, if the data processed was collected within the territory or pertains to citizens of the country.

Data minimization

The principle of data minimization means that personal data collection, storage, and usage should be limited to what is necessary for specific, explicit, and legitimate purposes. It implies that an entity (like a company or organization) should only collect, process, and store the minimum amount of data required to fulfill its purpose and nothing more. Related concepts are those of the data being *adequate* (for its purpose), *relevant* (to the purpose), and *limited* (to what is needed). Data Minimization is a requirement in many regulations and a good practice.

Accountability

This means an organization is responsible for the personal information under its control. Under many regulations, it means that organizations must not only comply with data protection principles but also demonstrate that they comply. For example, with documentation (of their data processing activities), the use of privacy-by-design principles, carrying out Data Protection Impact Assessments (DPIAs), the appointment of a DPO, or the provision of training and awareness for staff.

Special categories of data and group privacy

Many legislations define special categories of data that are particularly sensitive. For example, the special categories of personal data specifically mentioned by the GDPR are:

- Racial or ethnic origin
- Political opinions
- Religious or philosophical beliefs
- Trade union membership
- Genetic data
- Biometric data (where used for identification purposes)

- Health data
- Data concerning a person's sex life or sexual orientation.

As you can see, this type of data involves a high risk for discrimination. Therefore, the special categories of data are strongly connected to the concept of *Group Privacy*. Many legislations are designed not only to protect individual rights but also the rights of groups, be they racial, religious, political, or other. This is particularly relevant in the era of big data, where aggregated datasets can reveal information about groups that wouldn't be discernible from individual data points. For instance, analyzing aggregated health data might reveal disparities in health outcomes for certain racial or ethnic groups.

Storage limitation

This is another concept that protects Data Subjects. In simple terms, you should not keep personal data longer than needed. Once the stated purpose for which the data was collected has been fulfilled, the data should either be deleted or anonymized. For instance, if you're an online retailer and you collect a customer's delivery address to ship them a product, you should not keep that address indefinitely after the product has been delivered, unless there is a legitimate reason to do so (e.g., the customer has an account with you and will likely order again, or for tax reporting purposes).

Disposal

Disposal is a critical aspect of data lifecycle management and plays a key role in maintaining compliance with privacy laws and regulations. For instance, the *Storage Limitation* may require the deletion of the data. Another case is when an individual exercises their "right to be forgotten" (or "right to erasure"). Under many regulations, organizations must dispose of the data to ensure it cannot be recovered or reconstructed.

Disposal sounds easy – just delete it, right? In practice, it is often quite an elaborate process. Data disposal can involve methods such as:

- *Physical Destruction:* For physical media like paper or disks, this could involve shredding, pulverizing, or incinerating.

- *Digital Deletion:* For data stored electronically, simply deleting files or reformatting drives is often not sufficient, as data can often be recovered. Instead, secure deletion methods should be used that overwrite the data.

- *Degaussing:* For magnetic media, a degausser can be used to scramble the data beyond recognition.

- *Cryptographic Erasure:* If data was encrypted when stored, disposing of the cryptographic keys can render the data unreadable.

Proper disposal is important not only for maintaining privacy and compliance with regulations but also for mitigating the risk of data breaches.

Public interest

In the context of data privacy regulations, *public interest* refers to activities or actions that deliver benefits or protections for society at large. Under certain regulations, the concept of public interest is a lawful basis for processing personal data. This means that organizations can process personal data without obtaining individual consent if the processing is necessary for performing a task in the public interest or in the exercise of official authority vested in the data controller. For example, public health initiatives, such as tracking and containing infectious diseases (e.g., COVID-19), can be considered in the public interest. Similarly, activities like crime prevention or public safety measures are often conducted in the public interest. However, what exactly constitutes "public interest" can be a complex legal question and may vary between different legal jurisdictions. There's often a balance to be struck between the public interest and individual privacy rights.

Legitimate interest

Many regulations mention *legitimate interest* as one of the legal bases that allow for the processing of personal data. What does this mean? According to GDPR, data processing is lawful if it is "necessary for the purposes of the legitimate interests pursued by the controller or by a third party, except where such interests are overridden by the interests or fundamental rights and freedoms of the data subject which require protection of personal data."

Depending on the jurisdiction, the legitimate interests of a company could cover a wide range of situations. For example, a business might have a legitimate interest in processing personal data for fraud prevention (i.e., to verify identities and prevent fraudulent activities), direct marketing (market products to existing customers), IT and network security (ensure the security of its IT infrastructure) or reporting and analytics (to understand customer behavior and improve products or services).

So, the definition is perhaps, unfortunately, for data subjects, rather broad. However, even when a business identifies a legitimate interest, it still needs to conduct a *"Legitimate Interests Assessment"* (LIA), which is a form of risk assessment to balance its interests against the individual's interests, rights, and freedoms. It is not allowed if the processing would unfairly go against what is right and best for the individual. For example, if processing personal data for direct marketing would cause unwarranted harm to individuals, this would override the business's legitimate interests.

Data portability

Data portability is a right that allows individuals to receive personal data they have provided to a data controller in a structured, commonly used, and machine-readable format, and to transmit that data to another controller. It increases control over personal data, promotes competition and innovation, and enables data sharing for personal benefit.

For example, you might use a social media platform, and over time, you post photos, update statuses, like pages, and build a network of friends. If you decided to switch to a new social media platform, under the right to data portability, you could request a copy of all your personal data from the first platform in a structured, commonly used, and machine-readable format. Then, you could upload this data to the new platform, making the switch easier.

Profiling

Profiling can involve analyses of personal preferences, behaviors, interests, locations, and movements. It is commonly used in a variety of areas, including marketing, human resources, healthcare, and risk assessment. For example, profiling might be used to send targeted advertisements, predict future behavior, or make decisions about a person's eligibility for a service. Some regulations restrict the use of profiling.

Data Protection as a human right

Data protection is increasingly recognized as a fundamental human right (for example, in the GDPR). As our lives become more digitized and large amounts of personal data are processed and shared across the Internet, our data is an increasingly important part of ourselves.

In the text of GDPR, it is explicitly stated that "The processing of personal data should be designed to serve mankind. The right to the protection of personal data is not an absolute right; it must be considered in relation to its function in society and be balanced against other fundamental rights, in accordance with the principle of proportionality."

Other jurisdictions around the world also have laws and regulations that recognize the importance of data protection as a human right. For example, the California Consumer Privacy Act (CCPA) gives residents of California the right to know what personal data is being collected about them, the right to delete personal data held by businesses, and the right to opt-out of the sale of their personal data. The United Nations' Universal Declaration of Human Rights doesn't specifically mention data protection, but it does enshrine the right to privacy, of which data protection is a key component. This is often cited in discussions about data protection as a human right.

As AI is rapidly becoming commonplace, there are ongoing discussions globally about how to ensure effective data protection in AI and machine learning.

PIAs and DPIAs

PIA stands for Privacy Impact Assessment and DPIA stands for Data Protection Impact Assessment. These are tools used to identify and reduce the privacy risks of entities by analyzing the personal data that is processed and the policies in place to protect the data.

A *Privacy Impact Assessment* (PIA): A PIA is a process that assists organizations in identifying and minimizing the privacy risks of new projects or policies. PIAs help ensure that privacy protections are built into technology from the start and not as an afterthought.

A *Data Protection Impact Assessment* (DPIA): A DPIA is a specific requirement under the EU's General Data Protection Regulation (GDPR). DPIAs are required when data processing, particularly using new technologies, is likely to result in a high risk to the rights and freedoms of natural persons. This process involves systematically considering the potential impact that a project or initiative might have on people's privacy and includes measures to mitigate identified risks. A DPIA should describe the processing operations, the purposes of the processing, assess the necessity and proportionality of the processing operations in relation to the purposes, assess the risks to individuals, and describe the measures in place to address risk, including security and to demonstrate compliance. Therefore, DPIA is a special type of PIA used primarily in the context of GDPR.

Right to erasure / Right to be forgotten

This is one of the rights of citizens in many regulations: organizations can be requested to erase the data of a particular subject. This includes erasure from all backups as well, so this will have technical implications for the design of applications and management of data systems. The requirement to be able to perform this deletion thoroughly and reliably will likely have implications on the design of data operations in the first place.

Automated decision making

Automated decision-making refers to decisions made without human intervention, typically using algorithms or machine learning models. These decisions are often based on personal data collected about an individual. Automated decision-making can be beneficial in many contexts, making processes more efficient and eliminating human biases. However, it also raises significant privacy and ethical concerns. In fact, it may introduce new biases and unfairness.

Risk

The risk that data carries can be a criterion in determining the requirements or procedures to follow. Some regulations define types of *high-risk data* that require different safeguards and different procedures in case of a data breach.

Motivations behind data privacy regulations

Why do governments create privacy laws? What is the goal? The primary motivation behind data privacy regulations is the protection of individuals' fundamental rights in an increasingly digital world. While the Internet and digital technologies offer countless benefits, they also present significant challenges to privacy. The scale and speed of data collection, along with the ability to analyze and share data instantly and widely, can expose individuals to potential harm.

Data privacy regulations aim to balance the opportunities and benefits of innovation and technological advancements with the need to safeguard individual rights. Protecting personal data should not stifle innovation but rather stimulate the development of privacy-enhancing technologies and foster trust in digital services.

Regulations also aim to create legal certainty and a level playing field for businesses. In a global digital market, having a clear and harmonized set of rules helps ensure fair competition and fosters economic growth.

Beyond the legal considerations, data privacy also involves important ethical and societal considerations. Ethically, the respect for privacy is seen as respecting human dignity. It's about the right of individuals to control their personal information and to decide who can collect their data, how it is used, and with whom it is shared.

Societally, privacy helps to establish boundaries between individuals and organizations, contributing to the formation of a healthy and democratic society. It allows individuals to create and maintain a space for themselves, enabling them to communicate freely and participate in political and social activities without fear of surveillance or repercussion.

In the era of Big Data, these considerations become even more critical. With vast amounts of data being collected and processed, the power asymmetries between individuals and those collecting data can lead to potential misuse and harm, ranging from discrimination to manipulation.

Societal considerations

Data privacy has vast societal implications. As more and more of our personal data finds its way online and around the world, understanding and addressing these implications has become more crucial than ever. Perhaps one of the most apparent societal considerations of data privacy is its connection with individual autonomy and human rights. Privacy is often associated with personal freedom – the right to seclude information about oneself and, thereby, reveal oneself selectively. However, this personal freedom can be at risk with the vast quantity of data being collected by businesses, governments, and other entities. If not done with consent or transparently, the collection of personal data may undermine personal autonomy, infringe upon the individual's right to privacy, and even pose risks to other rights, such as freedom of expression and association.

Another key societal consideration revolves around the potential for discrimination and bias. Automated decision-making and profiling, for instance, can perpetuate social inequalities if not properly managed. They can lead to unfair outcomes, especially when algorithms use sensitive information like race, gender, or socioeconomic status as factors in decision-making. This can inadvertently disadvantage certain groups of people, perpetuating societal disparities and prejudice.

Data privacy also has significant implications for democracy and governance. Governments' use of data can lead to surveillance if not properly controlled, infringing upon the privacy rights of citizens. There are many analyses of the potential influence of the 2016 US elections through social networks, profiling individual citizens and targeting them with specific online content to influence their political viewpoints. This can ultimately threaten democratic values, such as the freedom of speech and the right to a private life. Moreover, the lack of privacy can deter people from expressing their opinions openly, fearing potential repercussions, thereby curtailing democratic discourse.

Economically, data privacy is an integral part of consumer trust in the digital economy. If businesses are transparent about their data collection practices and take steps to protect user data, consumers are more likely to trust them. In contrast, data breaches cause reputational damage and financial losses for businesses, impacting the overall health of the digital economy. Respecting data privacy becomes a good business practice. It should be considered as part of an organization's Environmental, Social, and Governance (ESG) commitments.

Addressing data privacy concerns at the level of society requires a multidisciplinary approach that combines legal, ethical, technical, and societal perspectives. Educating the public about data privacy issues is crucial to fostering a culture of privacy and ensuring that individuals can make informed decisions about their data. In the long term, a balanced approach to data privacy that respects individual rights and enables the benefits of data analysis could help create a more equitable and privacy-respecting digital society. In Chapter 3, we will look at a number of examples to see how different countries try to achieve that, including in regulations such as the General Data Protection Regulation (GDPR) in the European Union, the California Consumer Privacy Act (CCPA) in the United States and others around the globe.

CHAPTER 2

About Personal Data

Personal data is at the core of this book. It is the main subject of data privacy regulations. As a cornerstone of many modern digital services, personal data is an increasingly valuable asset. However, personal data can be a toxic asset, too. It introduces significant risks for the organization while at the same time being subject to mandatory retention in some cases. As organizations continue to harness the power of personal data, it becomes imperative to understand its intricacies and the obligations that come with its handling.

To design a data privacy strategy, as we will do in Chapter 5, we need to first thoroughly understand personal data. It is safe to say that many companies handle personal data without realizing it.

In this chapter, we delve into the scope and nature of personal data, explore the principles and best practices for its protection, and discuss the challenges and considerations with emerging technologies and platforms.

Defining personal data

We can all think of obvious examples of personal data: a name, an address, a date of birth, and even someone's Netflix browsing history. However, there are many more nuanced cases and grey areas. An exact definition of *personal data* is not all that easy and, in fact, differs in various global regulations. As a Data Privacy strategy designer, you want to be sure to cover all the data that might possibly put the organization at risk, so definitions are important and precision matters. Sometimes, it is not about one single piece of data, but a combination of pieces that can lead to identification. Time and location matter too, as we will see.

To start our exploration, observe that the term *personal data* has two components: "personal" and "data."

Personal

Let us first look at the definition of *personal* in different regulations:

The EU General Data Protection Regulation (GDPR), Article 4(1):

> "...personal data' means any information relating to an **identified or identifiable natural person** ('data subject'); an identifiable natural person is one who can be identified, directly or indirectly, in particular by

reference to an identifier such as a name, an identification number, location data, an online identifier or to one or more factors specific to the physical, physiological, genetic, mental, economic, cultural or social identity of that natural person;"

We will look later into the concept of identifiability.

The California Consumer Privacy Act (CCPA), Section 1798.140 (o) (1):

"(o) (1) "Personal information" means information that identifies, relates to, describes, is reasonably capable of being associated with, or could reasonably be linked, directly or indirectly, with a particular consumer or household. Personal information includes, but is not limited to, the following if it identifies, relates to, describes, is reasonably capable of being associated with, or could be reasonably linked, directly or indirectly, with **a particular consumer or household**...."

CCPA's definition of personal information is broader than the GDPR's definition of personal data, as it also covers information associated with households, not just individuals.

The Lei Geral de Proteção de Dados Pessoais in Brazil states ,in Article 5(I):

(Translated from Portuguese)

"Personal data: information regarding **an identified or identifiable natural person**."

This definition is somewhat more general than its counterparts, GDPR and CCPA. Still, the fundamental idea is the same: any information that can identify or be used to identify a natural person.

South Africa's Protection of Personal Information Act (POPIA), Section 1 says:

> "'personal information' means information relating to an identifiable, living, natural person, and where it is applicable, an identifiable, existing juristic person."

Interestingly, this law extends the definition to include *juristic person*, that is, legal entities such as companies.

Data

Next, let's look at the types of data that constitute personal data according to different regulations.

GDPR Article 4(1) states:

> "...personal data' means any information relating to an identified or identifiable natural person ('data subject'); an identifiable natural person is one who can be identified, directly or indirectly, in particular by reference to an identifier such as a **name, an identification number, location data, an online identifier or to one or more factors specific to the physical, physiological, genetic, mental, economic, cultural or social identity of that natural person;"**

In defining the term "identifiable," the GDPR gives concrete examples of data elements that are personal data. In practice, these also include all data that are or can be assigned to a person in any kind of way. For example, the telephone, credit card, or personnel number of a person, account data, a car's license plate, appearance, customer number, or address are all personal data.

CCPA 1798.140 (o) (1) contains a long list of examples as well:

A. Identifiers such as a real name, alias, postal address, unique personal identifier, online identifier, internet protocol address, email address, account name, social security number, driver's license number, passport number, or other similar identifiers.

B. Any categories of personal information described in subdivision (e) of Section 1798.80.

C. Characteristics of protected classifications under California or federal law.

D. Commercial information, including records of personal property, products or services purchased, obtained, or considered, or other purchasing or consuming histories or tendencies.

E. Biometric information.

F. Internet or other electronic network activity information, including, but not limited to, browsing history, search history, and information regarding a consumer's interaction with an internet website, application, or advertisement.

G. Geolocation data.

H. Audio, electronic, visual, thermal, olfactory, or similar information.

I. Professional or employment-related information.

J. Education information, defined as information that is not publicly available personally identifiable information as defined in the Family Educational Rights and Privacy Act (20 U.S.C. Sec. 1232g; 34 C.F.R. Part 99).

K. Inferences drawn from any of the information identified in this subdivision to create a profile about a consumer reflecting the consumer's preferences, characteristics, psychological trends, predispositions, behavior, attitudes, intelligence, abilities, and aptitudes.

Some of these data elements, such as geolocation data, have significant consequences, as we will see later. Internet-related digital information such as browser history (i.e., "cookies") is also something we shall look at later in more detail. Sub-section K, which explicitly includes the concept of a profile of people reflecting their preferences, is also noteworthy.

CCPA Sections 1798.140 (o) (2) and (o) (3) also provide clarity of what is *not* included:

> (2) "Personal information" does not include publicly available information. For purposes of this paragraph, "publicly available" means information that is lawfully made available from federal, state, or local government records. "Publicly available" does not mean biometric information collected by a business about a consumer without the consumer's knowledge.

> (3) "Personal information" does not include consumer information that is deidentified or aggregate consumer information.

If you bought a home in the US, the sales record is publicly listed. Your phone number may also be listed unless you choose not to. Your car's registration is made public by the Department of Motor Vehicles. These are, therefore, not included. In fact, many companies across the US make money selling such data.

Singapore's Personal Data Protection Act 2012 (PDPA) defines 'personal data' in Section 2(1):

> "'personal data' means data, whether true or not, about an individual who can be identified — (a) from that data; or (b) from that data and other information to which the organization has or is likely to have access;"

The concept of combining data from different sources to allow identification of a person is an important addition, and something that is not trivial to see right away. It requires looking holistically at all the data your organization collects. Furthermore, the clause "whether true or not" is an interesting addition.

South Africa's Protection of Personal Information Act (POPIA), Section 1 lists various data types:

> a) information relating to the race, gender, sex, pregnancy, marital status, national, ethnic or social origin, colour, sexual orientation, age, physical or mental health, well-being, disability, religion, conscience, belief, culture, language and birth of the person; (b) information relating to the education or the medical, financial, criminal or employment history of the person; (c) any identifying number, symbol, e-mail address, physical address, telephone number, location information, online identifier or other particular assignment to the person; (d) the biometric information of the person; (e) the personal opinions, views or preferences of the person; (f) correspondence sent by the person that is implicitly or explicitly of a private or confidential nature or further correspondence that would reveal the contents of the original correspondence; (g) the views or opinions of another Individual about the person; and (h) the name of the person if it appears with other personal information relating to the person or if the disclosure of the name itself would reveal information about the person.

This broad definition covers a wide array of data, and it is quite expansive in terms of the types of information it encompasses, including biometric information, personal opinions, and, interestingly, the views of others about the person. This can be obvious if one were to compile a database of opinions about a certain person with the intent of forming a profile about the person. But what about an online discussion forum that includes threads of comments where users comment on other's opinions and, implicitly or explicitly, express an opinion about those other users?

Challenges in recognizing personal data

Some of the examples of personal data listed above are straightforward. Others are less obvious, and especially in the context of the daily operations of an organization, it is easy to forget that some data may be personal or sensitive.

Let's say we own an automobile manufacturing company. While our vehicles aren't equipped with advanced self-driving technology, we do collect mechanical data from the cars to support customers in letting them know in advance about problems with their car and improve our technology, such as the braking system and collision warning feature. We download this data from the car whenever it is serviced.

The data includes location (GPS) and operational data, such as speed at a given time. At first glance, this data might appear harmless to our engineers. However, the combination of location and speed can reveal if a driver was breaking the law at any particular time. The driver can be identified using the vehicle's registration number and by cross-referencing our customer database that tracks car sales and service appointments.

Now, imagine our customer is embroiled in a tumultuous divorce as their spouse accuses them of infidelity. Suddenly, the location data can transform into intensely personal information. Or imagine a bank robbery was committed in the area. The location data of the car at that particular time may now constitute an alibi for the customer (or, conversely, make them a suspect). Under several regulations, this data may now, in fact, qualify as *sensitive data*.

Obtaining data from cars, thermostats, video cameras at your front door, sports watches, or other accessories is now commonplace. Either to allow remote operation of the devices, to provide warnings (e.g., a smoke detector), or to provide additional services such as a weekly exercise report or your car's energy consumption. Intelligent fridges exist now that can tell you about their contents remotely – a handy feature when you are in the supermarket deciding what to buy. Your organization may lose out against the competition if you don't follow this trend and leverage the data to provide modern services to your customers. Yet the data collected can often be classified as personal, especially when different data elements are combined.

Data about digital behavior, such as browsing history, is another challenging aspect. Let's imagine a new scenario in which we operate a fashion business and sell products online through our e-commerce website. We collect data through "cookies," some of which are necessary to operate the site (e.g., keeping track of the customer's virtual shopping cart), and some are used to provide a better experience (e.g., products that are relevant to you, such as women's clothing rather than men's or children's). Our marketing team also uses the data to design new marketing campaigns. They are interested in customers who browse multiple types of products. For instance, female customers in their forties who also browse children's clothes sometimes, or young people who buy jeans but also sports attire. The purpose is to co-brand or style products that go together.

Although the Data Privacy Officer has reviewed the data collected and the purpose of doing so, the Marketing department often comes up with creative new ideas and asks the website engineers to store some additional cookies. They decide to use the data to identify young women who have browsed for baby clothes and maternity dresses and provide their addresses to an events management company to invite them to a special marketing event. They do not inform the Data Privacy

Officer about this new use of the data. Obviously, they are not being respectful of personal data and may well cause harm to the organization.

Collecting information about online behavior is particularly tricky because collecting it is so easy. Every link you click on, the amount of time your cursor hovers over an image, the time you spend on a page, and every letter typed can be collected easily and at almost no cost. There are no technical costs. But the cost to your organization, in terms of risk and obligations that come with ownership of this data, is definitely not negligible.

Sensitive data

Most regulations, including the GDPR, the CCPA, South Africa's POPIA, Brazil's LGPD, and even as far back as Australia's Privacy Act of 1988, recognize a separate category of "sensitive personal data." The idea is that this type of data presents a higher risk to an individual's fundamental rights and freedoms, particularly the right to privacy, and therefore needs stricter regulation.

The definition of sensitive personal data differs from country to country, but it often includes information about:

- Racial or ethnic origin
- Political opinions
- Religious or philosophical beliefs

- Trade union membership
- Genetic or biometric data
- Health information
- Sexual orientation
- Criminal convictions or offenses.

However, there may be other categories. For example, China's Personal Information Protection Law (PIPL) classifies the personal information of children under the age of 14 as sensitive data.

The misuse, unauthorized access, or disclosure of such information could lead to significant harm for the individual concerned, including discrimination, stigmatization, damage to reputation, or even potential for harm or violence. Because of these risks, many data protection laws impose stricter rules, often requiring explicit consent from the data subject and limiting the circumstances in which such data can be processed.

For instance, in GDPR, Article 9 says:

1. Processing of personal data revealing racial or ethnic origin, political opinions, religious or philosophical beliefs, or trade union membership, and the processing of genetic data, biometric data for the purpose of uniquely identifying a natural person, data concerning health or data concerning a natural person's sex life or sexual orientation shall be prohibited.

2. Paragraph 1 shall not apply if one of the following applies:

- the data subject has given explicit consent to the processing of those personal data for one or more specified purposes, except where Union or Member State law provide that the prohibition referred to in paragraph 1 may not be lifted by the data subject;

- processing is necessary for the purposes of carrying out the obligations and exercising specific rights of the controller or of the data subject in the field of employment and social security and social protection law in so far as it is authorised by Union or Member State law or a collective agreement pursuant to Member State law providing for appropriate safeguards for the fundamental rights and the interests of the data subject;

- ...

(list continues with more exceptions)

Additionally, organizations that process sensitive data must ensure they have appropriate safeguards in place to protect this data and notify data subjects of their rights. This includes their rights to access, rectify, erase, restrict, or object to the processing of their data.

By having a separate category for sensitive data, the laws aim to ensure that this type of data is given a higher level of protection to minimize the potential harm that could result from its misuse.

The definition of personal data varies across different regulations and different countries. Many regulations recognize a special category of "sensitive data" that poses a higher risk to the rights of individuals and, therefore, is subject to stricter rules. Identifying all uses of personal or sensitive data in your organization's operations is often far from easy. Creative uses of data are tempting, and misuse of personal data can happen easily.

Principles for protecting personal data

The handling of personal data is guided by several key principles, which serve as the foundation for most data protection regulations worldwide. In Chapter 3, we will review different regulations around the world and will see these principles come by repeatedly. Understanding these principles is critical to the development of effective data protection strategies.

Purpose

What are we collecting the data for? We need to be clear about this because it makes a big difference in the way we need to treat the data.

In the context of data privacy, the term "purpose" refers to the specific, explicit, and legitimate reasons for which personal data is collected and processed. A fundamental principle of most data protection laws is that the purpose for data collection and processing should be clear. In most cases, it must be made transparent to the individual from whom the data is being collected.

Defining the *purpose* is essential for a number of reasons:

- Limitation: By specifying the purpose of data collection, organizations ensure they don't collect more data than necessary or use it in ways that the individual has not consented to.

- Transparency: It ensures that individuals are aware of how their data will be used. We will talk more about this in the next chapter.

- Security: It helps organizations determine the appropriate security measures needed to protect the data, as different types of data may require different levels of protection.

A common requirement in regulations is a *purpose limitation*. This principle requires that personal data must be collected for specified, explicit, and legitimate purposes and not further processed in a manner incompatible with those purposes. In practice, this means that organizations need to be clear about why they're collecting data and what they're going to use it for. They must not use the data for other purposes that the individual has not consented to or that are not legally justified.

Data minimization

Data minimization is the principle that organizations should only collect and process the personal data that is necessary for the specified purpose.

For example, the General Data Protection Regulation (GDPR) in Europe states in Article 5(1)(c):

> Personal data shall be:
>
> (c) adequate, relevant and limited to what is necessary in relation to the purposes for which they are processed ('data minimisation');

This means businesses cannot store more personal data than they need, nor can they keep it for longer than necessary. The regulation also requires data controllers to provide clear retention periods for the data they store or criteria used to determine those periods.

This principle helps reduce the risks associated with data processing activities by limiting the amount of data collected and processed. Data minimization encourages organizations to critically evaluate their data and align their data collection practices with their legitimate needs.

Accuracy

This principle means that data should be accurate and kept up to date. Inaccurate data should be erased or rectified without delay. The idea is that keeping out-of-date information about a person treats them unfairly. Ensuring the accuracy of data is a requirement for data controllers under many regulations.

For example, in GDPR:

> Personal data shall be:
>
> (d) accurate and, where necessary, kept up to date; every reasonable step must be taken to ensure that personal data that are inaccurate, having regard to the purposes for which they are processed, are erased or rectified without delay ('accuracy');"

In addition, some regulations grant data subjects the right to correct incomplete, inaccurate, or out-of-date data.

Storage

Obviously, your personal data needs to be stored somewhere. While some regulations include personal data in any form, be it digital, on paper, or even other forms, for this section we will focus on the storage of digital data.

Data storage may seem like a mundane and boring issue. Still, it is important with respect to data privacy because many regulations stipulate specific requirements for security and other measures to be in place to safeguard people's personal data.

The most obvious connection to data privacy is the *storage limitation* that features in many regulations.

The GDPR, in Article 5(1) states:

> Personal data shall be: (e) kept in a form which permits identification of data subjects for no longer than is necessary for the purposes for which the personal data are processed; personal data may be stored for longer periods insofar as the personal data will be processed solely for archiving purposes in the public interest, scientific or historical research purposes or statistical purposes [...]

The Personal Data Protection Act (PDPA) in Singapore similarly states that organizations may only retain personal data for as long as it is necessary to fulfill the purpose for which it was collected. If the data is no longer needed for that purpose, it should be destroyed or anonymized.

Brazil's Lei Geral de Proteção de Dados (LGPD) also includes data minimization and storage limitation.

> "Personal data can only be used for the purpose for which it was collected, and it must be deleted after it has served its purpose, unless there's a legal ground for its maintenance, like compliance with a legal obligation, study by a research entity, or credit protection."

The concept of data storage is strongly connected to *IT security*. For instance, the California Consumer Privacy Act (CCPA) states businesses are required to implement and maintain reasonable security procedures and practices to protect consumers' data. Although it does not directly impose limitations on the duration of data storage, one could say a data storage limitation is implicit since storing the data longer than it is needed would bring unnecessary security risks.

The requirement to delete a specific part of data that was collected at a certain time can be challenging. For a programmer designing an IT system, it may seem logical to store various data elements collected about one and the same customer in a single record. That could become problematic, however, if different elements were collected at different times and for different purposes. Another challenge is backups – although a useful practice to avoid loss of data, it also means that deletions must be made on all existing backups.

These concepts show up in various regulations. They overlap with the concepts of Storage, IT security, and Accuracy. Personal data must be processed and stored in a manner that ensures appropriate security, including protection against unauthorized or unlawful processing, accidental loss, destruction, or damage.

Somewhat related to the purpose limitation is the *storage limitation* that features in many regulations. The storage limitation principle relates to the retention of personal data. It mandates that personal data should be kept in a form that permits the identification of data subjects for no longer than is necessary for the purposes for which the personal data are processed. In other words, once the data has served its purpose, it should be securely deleted or anonymized.

However, storage limitation often needs to be balanced against other legal obligations, which may include mandatory retention policies. Mandatory retention policies are requirements set by law, regulation, or industry standards that certain types of data be retained for a set period. For example, financial institutions may be required to keep customer transaction data for a certain number of years for auditing and regulatory purposes.

In cases where there is a conflict between the principle of storage limitation and a mandatory retention policy, the latter typically takes precedence. The GDPR, for instance, explicitly recognizes in Article 5(1)(e) that data may be stored longer if used to comply with a legal obligation.

Nevertheless, organizations must still ensure that they are only keeping personal data necessary to comply with the legal obligation. Furthermore, they must continue to apply appropriate safeguards to protect the data during this retention period. Once the period stipulated by the mandatory retention policy expires, the data should then be disposed of in accordance with the principle of storage limitation.

Challenges posed by emerging technologies

Emerging technologies, such as Internet of Things (IoT) devices, wearables, social media platforms, and AI-powered tools and applications, present unique challenges for personal data protection. These technologies generate vast amounts of data, often in real-time, and can provide detailed insights into an individual's behaviors, preferences, and habits.

These tools have shaped society, sometimes making it harder for customers to identify their data choices and tempting companies to collect more data. Take social networks, for instance. Young people love to share moments of their lives – a party they are attending, a piece of chocolate cake they eat, or their new haircut. They are sharing a lot of data while doing so. While users provide the data voluntarily, much of it is collected passively as users interact with the platform. This can lead to the creation of detailed profiles, which can be used for targeted advertising and, in some cases, be manipulated for nefarious purposes.

It is very reassuring to enable your thermostat, smoke alarm, or doorbell to provide notifications to your cell phone when you are not home – they likely use servers run by the manufacturer to store and transfer the data. Modern sports watches can keep track of your vitals and performance and keep a record of it on the organization's servers. The list goes on.

The massive adoption of these technologies in our culture makes it tempting for consumers to click "yes" on the Terms and Conditions of products and services. The value of their consent is increasingly questionable. Much of the data can be highly sensitive and create significant risks if not properly protected. The changing nature of computing, with data moving between cloud-based services and connected devices, means traditional concepts and architectures for IT security may no longer be sufficient.

We have seen several key principles for data protection: the purpose of collected data, the need for accuracy, data minimization, and storage of data (and restrictions to that). These principles will come back frequently when we study some examples of global data privacy regulations in Chapter 3 and are also key elements in a strategy for data privacy, as we will see in Chapter 5.

CHAPTER 3

The Global Landscape of Data Privacy Regulations

This chapter will discuss important privacy regulations in different areas of the world, with examples from North America, Europe, South America, Africa, and Asia. We will compare these regulations to one another. It is not a comprehensive list. We chose these specific countries because together, they represent a good range of the types of regulations you might encounter. Some countries have strict data protection laws, others only minimal regulation. Some laws are at the level of a state or province. Some are national or regional. Some have broad coverage, while others focus on a specific aspect.

The chapter discusses the scope and applicability of these regulations and provides insights into their similarities and differences. It also explores the extraterritorial reach of certain data privacy regulations. It explains how organizations that process the personal data of individuals residing in a specific jurisdiction may still be subject to compliance requirements under those regulations, even if the organization is located elsewhere. These are important considerations when dealing with personal data internationally.

The information in this chapter is not meant to be legal. The goal of this chapter is to understand the *spirit* of the regulations, become acquainted with a certain kind of thought process, and apply this process when designing a corporate data privacy strategy.

The European Union

Perhaps the most famous of all privacy regulations, the General Data Protection Regulation (GDPR) is a data protection directive enacted by the European Union (EU) that came into effect on May 25, 2018.[1] GDPR was the first major comprehensive legal framework for data privacy. This comprehensive regulation sets a new global standard for privacy rights, security, and compliance. It has had enormous effects on the world, both in the practical sense and as an inspiration for the design of frameworks in other regions and nations.

Practically, it has major implications for European businesses and for international businesses collecting data

---

[1] For the official text, see: https://gdpr-info.eu/

about European Citizens. In terms of international businesses collecting data on EU citizens, the large social networks and cloud services providers such as Facebook and Google are the most visible of these. In fact, it applies to thousands of international companies. The desire to do business with the EU and collect data in the EU, including potentially personal data, led to several countries adopting privacy laws in or shortly after 2018 to qualify for trusted status for the EU.

This section will only talk about GDPR, but this is not the only European regulation relevant for Privacy. The older ePrivacy Directive[2] is still valid and relevant, in particular to using personal data in marketing and advertising (which is the business model of many "free" online platforms such as social networks). It will likely soon be replaced by a new ePrivacy regulation.[3] There are also national laws that complement the EU directives, such as Germany's Telecommunications Telemedia Data Protection Act (TTDSG).

---

[2] See: https://edps.europa.eu/data-protection/our-work/publications/legislation/directive-2009136ec_en

[3] See: https://data.consilium.europa.eu/doc/document/ST-6087-2021-INIT/en/pdf

Understanding the spirit of the GDPR

The objectives of GDPR are to strengthen individuals' data protection rights, establish clear rules for organizations handling personal data, promote transparency and accountability in data processing, and ensure a harmonized approach to data protection across the European Union.

A distinguishing feature of the GDPR is its broad scope, applying not only to EU-based companies but to all companies that process the personal data of EU residents, irrespective of the organization's location. There are strict rules on transferring data outside the EU. The basic idea here is that the level of protection granted to citizens should not diminish through the transfer of data elsewhere.

A further key concept is the (need for a) *legal basis* for processing data. Rather than just specifying what type of data processing is illegal, GDPR starts from the idea that any type of data collection or processing needs a valid reason (legal basis) to do so.

Material scope

The term "personal data" is defined broadly under the GDPR, and it includes any information related to a natural person (called a "data subject") that can be used to directly or indirectly identify that person. This can range from a name, a photo, an email address, bank details, posts on social networking websites, medical information, or even a computer IP address.

Article 4 (1):

> 'personal data' means any information relating to an identified or identifiable natural person ('data subject'); an identifiable natural person is one who can be identified, directly or indirectly, in particular by reference to an identifier such as a name, an identification number, location data, an online identifier or to one or more factors specific to the physical, physiological, genetic, mental, economic, cultural or social identity of that natural person;

The GDPR establishes several key principles in relation to data processing. These include lawfulness, fairness, and transparency; purpose limitation; data minimization; accuracy; storage limitation; integrity and confidentiality (security); and accountability. These principles lay the groundwork for the rights of data subjects and the responsibilities of data controllers and processors.

GDPR distinguishes *Controllers* and *Processors* of the data, and that may have implications for your organization if you outsource some of your data processing or if you obtain (access to) data from a third party. Parts of the GDPR may or may not apply to you, depending on the roles that you take.

It is also interesting to look at which types of data are not included:

- Anonymous data
- Deceased persons' data
- Household or personal activities (non-commercial)

As a regional legislation, the GDPR also exempts the use of data for national security and law enforcement, as these are regulated by each member state individually.

Territorial scope

The GDPR applies to all organizations, regardless of location, that process the personal data of individuals residing in the EU if the processing activities are related to *offering goods or services* to EU citizens (irrespective of whether payment is required) or *monitoring behavior* within the EU. The GDPR also applies to organizations outside the EU if they process the personal data of EU residents on behalf of an organization located within the EU.

Requirements

Data controllers, the entities that determine the purposes and means of processing personal data, have an array of obligations under the GDPR. These include ensuring that data processing is *lawful*, *fair*, and *transparent*. The processing is only lawful if it meets one of the several conditions set out in the GDPR, including the data subject's *consent*, the *necessity* of processing for a contract with the data subject, *compliance* with a legal obligation, *protection* of vital interests, *necessity* for public interest or official authority, and legitimate interests pursued by the controller or a third party.

In addition, data controllers have an obligation to minimize data collection and retention. They are required to keep personal data accurate and up-to-date, rectifying or deleting inaccurate data without delay. Personal data may only be kept in a form that permits the identification of data subjects for as long as necessary for the purposes for which the data were collected. The controller must also ensure the security of personal data, using appropriate technical and organizational measures, and report any breaches to the supervisory authority and, in certain cases, to the data subject.

The accountability principle, a new addition to EU data protection law under the GDPR, mandates that the controller be responsible for and able to demonstrate compliance with, the principles relating to processing of personal data. This can involve implementing data protection policies, documenting processing activities, conducting data protection impact assessments for higher-risk processing, and appointing a data protection officer in certain cases.

Another notable requirement is the appointment of a Data protection Officer or DPO if you are a public authority, carry out large-scale systematic monitoring, or carry out large-scale processing of special categories of data or data relating to criminal convictions and offenses.

Two other requirements are:

- *Records of Processing Activities*: you must keep records of your processing activities if you have more than 250 employees, or if your processing activities could result in a risk to the rights and freedoms of data subjects, are not occasional, or involve certain types of sensitive personal data.

- *Security Measures*: You must implement appropriate security measures to protect personal data, taking into account the state of the art, the costs of implementation, the nature, scope, context, and purposes of processing, and the risk to individuals.

The GDPR also includes a requirement for *Breach Notifications*. There are requirements to notify the authorities and requirements to notify the data subjects.

Article 33 (1):

> In the case of a personal data breach, the controller shall without undue delay and, where feasible, not later than 72 hours after having become aware of it, notify the personal data breach to the supervisory authority

competent [...] unless the personal data breach is unlikely to result in a risk to the rights and freedoms of natural persons.

Article 34 (1):

When the personal data breach is likely to result in a high risk to the rights and freedoms of natural persons, the controller shall communicate the personal data breach to the data subject without undue delay.

Rights of data subjects

The GDPR has also enhanced the rights of data subjects, providing them greater control over their personal data. These rights include:

- the right to be informed about how personal data is used,

- the right to access one's personal data,

- the right to rectification if data is incorrect or incomplete,

- the right to erasure (also known as the "right to be forgotten"),

- the right to restrict the processing of personal data,

- the right to data portability,

- the right to object to processing,

- rights in relation to automated decision-making and profiling (e.g., by AI systems!)

Cross border transfers

Articles 45-50 in the GDPR are dedicated to the "Transfers of personal data to third countries or international organisations."

GDPR prohibits the transfer of personal data to countries outside the European Economic Area (EU member states plus Iceland, Liechtenstein, and Norway). These are referred to as cross-border or third-country transfers. The basic premise is that personal data should not be transferred to a country or international organization outside the EEA unless that country or organization ensures an adequate level of protection for the data.

Article 45 (1)

> A transfer of personal data to a third country or an international organisation may take place where the Commission has decided that the third country, a territory or one or more specified sectors within that third country, or the international organisation in question ensures an adequate level of protection. Such a transfer shall not require any specific authorisation.

The GDPR talks specifically about the criteria that define "adequate" protection. A number of countries have qualified for this exception, for instance, Switzerland, Canada, Argentina, Japan, and New Zealand. After Brexit, the UK has also been awarded adequacy status. If a country has not been deemed to provide an adequate level of protection, a data transfer may still take place if the data controller or processor has provided 'appropriate safeguards'.

In July 2023, the European Commission adopted its adequacy decision for the EU-US Decision Framework, which concludes that the "United States ensures an adequate level of protection – comparable to that of the European Union – for personal data transferred from the EU to US companies under the new framework. On the basis of the new adequacy decision, personal data can flow safely from the EU to US companies participating in the Framework, without having to put in place additional data protection safeguards."[4]

Enforcement

To ensure that these regulations are followed, the GDPR empowers data protection authorities to enforce these rules, with the potential for substantial penalties.

---

[4] https://ec.europa.eu/commission/presscorner/detail/en/ip_23_3721

Infringements of the basic principles for processing personal data, including conditions for consent, are subject to the highest tier of administrative fines. This could mean a fine of up to 20 million euros or, in the case of an undertaking, up to 4% of the total worldwide annual turnover of the preceding financial year, whichever is higher.

These fines are not theoretical. Since the adoption of GDPR, many companies have received large fines. In 2021, Amazon was fined €746 million for non-compliance with the GDPR. In May 2023, Facebook's owner, Meta, was fined €1.2 billion for improperly transferring data from the EU to the US. Google, H&M British Airways, and Marriott International have paid fines in the tens of millions of euros as well.

GDPR is a comprehensive law that takes serious effort to comply with. It has served as a model for many other regulations. It is far-reaching: it applies to those offering goods or services to EU citizens (irrespective of whether payment is required) and monitoring behavior that takes place within the EU. It contains a requirement to appoint a Data Privacy Officer (DPO) in some cases. One of the key concepts is that one must have a legal basis for processing data. It also has tough restrictions on Cross border transfers—moving personal data outside of the EU can be complex.

The United States

In the US, no general regulation exists at the federal level that would harmonize data protection across all states in the way that GDPR does for European countries. A general data protection regulation is being discussed, but some are skeptical that it will pass congress.

For the moment, regulation is different in all 50 states. As of 2023, only five States (California, Virginia, Colorado, Utah, and Connecticut) have general data protection laws in effect, although six more have adopted bills that will take effect somewhere in 2024-2026. Most states have their own regulation around data breach notifications.

Having said that, the US has a number of sector-specific laws at the federal level, such as financial institutions (Gramm-Leach-Billey Act), credit reporting (Fair Credit Reporting Act), healthcare (Health Insurance Portability and Accountability Act), as well as children's privacy (Children's Online Privacy Protection Act). And when it comes to data controlled by government agencies, privacy regulations have existed for a long time. The Privacy Act of 1974 was the first major act and was visionary at the time. An amendment in 1988 that included provision for computerized processing and the E-Government act of 2022 (in particular section 208.b on data privacy) bring the regulation further up to date with technological developments. These are designed only to regulate government agencies – they do not apply to businesses or academia.

This section will cover two privacy laws in the US, the California Consumer Privacy Act (CCPA) and the Health Insurance Portability and Accountability Act (HIPAA).

The California Consumer Privacy Act (CCPA)

The California Consumer Privacy Act (CCPA),[5] which came into effect on January 1, 2020, is one of the United States' most comprehensive data privacy laws, even though it only applies in one State! It was enacted to enhance privacy rights and consumer protection for residents of California. The CCPA is, in many ways, inspired by Europe's General Data Protection Regulation (GDPR), offering a similar range of privacy protections for Californians.

Scope

The CCPA applies to for-profit businesses that collect consumers' personal data and do business in California, regardless of whether the organization is based in California or even in the US. However, not all businesses are subject to the CCPA. To fall under its purview, a business must meet at least *one* of the following criteria:

---

[5] For the official text, see https://www.oag.ca.gov/privacy/ccpa

- Have annual gross revenues in excess of $25 million.

- Buy, receive, sell, or share the personal information of 50,000 or more consumers, households, or devices for commercial purposes.

- Derive 50% or more of their annual revenues from selling consumers' personal information.

Affiliated companies, such as parent companies or subsidiaries, are also subject to CCPA if the connection is strong enough (e.g., they control more than 50% of the shares), even if these parent or subsidiary companies themselves do not meet the criteria above.

Requirements

The requirements of the CCPA can be divided into two categories: obligations on businesses and rights of consumers. Businesses are required to *Inform Consumers* [of the fact that their data is being collected] before or at the point of data collection; Create Procedures *to respond* to consumer Requests; Obtain Explicit *Consent for Minors; Not Discriminate;* and *Train Employees.*

Rights of data subjects

Under the CCPA, consumers are granted the *Right to Know* what personal information businesses collect, use, share, or sell; the *Right to Delete* their information; the *Right to Opt-*

Out; The *Right to Non-Discrimination;* the *Right to Data Portability;* and the *Right to Opt-In for Minors.*

The US Health Insurance Portability and Accountability Act (HIPAA)

The Health Insurance Portability and Accountability Act (HIPAA)[6] is a federal law that was originally enacted by the United States Congress in 1996. It was augmented in 2000 by the Transaction Rule (which addressed issues introduced by electronic billing) and the Privacy rule of 2000 (which addresses the use and disclosure of individuals' health information and privacy rights for the subject to determine how their information is used) and the Security Rule of 2003 (that specifies how to operationalize technical and non-technical safeguards). Further legislation that amended the HIPAA are the Genetic Information Non-discrimination Act (GINA) and the Health Information Technology For Economic and Clinical Health Act (HITEC). Finally, the HIPAA Omnibus Final rule of 2013 served to make all the amendments permanent.

The HIPAA affects a wide range of healthcare and health-related activities in the US.

---

[6] See: https://www.healthit.gov/sites/default/files/rules-regulation/health-insurance-portability.pdf

Understanding the spirit of HIPAA

HIPAA aims to improve insurance portability and administrative simplification while also strengthening fraud prevention and ensuring the security and privacy of health data. HIPAA does not preempt stricter state laws. HIPAA serves as the "floor," not the ceiling.

Scope

HIPAA applies only to entities operating in the US. Originally, the law only applied to "covered entities" (i.e., health plans, doctors, etc.). As of 2009, the law also includes "business associates" (i.e., service providers that may access patient data).

In practice, this means a range of American healthcare providers and service providers, such as a billing company, a company that provides software for managing patient records, a law firm providing legal services to a healthcare provider, a consultant performing utilization reviews for a hospital, etc.

Requirements

The requirements of HIPAA can be broadly grouped into two main rules: the Privacy Rule and the Security Rule. The Privacy Rule establishes national standards for protecting individuals' medical records and other personal health information. It includes limits on the *use and disclosure* of Protected Health Information (PHI); it requires *written consent* from individuals before their PHI is used for purposes like marketing; it requires *training of employees* and the *appointment of a Privacy Officer*; and providing patients *with access* to their records and the ability to amend or correct inaccuracies.

The Security Rule deals specifically with Electronic Protected Health Information (ePHI). It contains three requirements: 1) *Administrative Safeguards:* policies and procedures designed to clearly show how the entity will comply with HIPAA. This includes the selection of a security officer, employee training, and access control; 2) *Physical Safeguards, which* include facility access controls, workstation, and device security measures; and 3) *Technical Safeguards.*

Data breach regulations

Most States in the US also have data breach laws that would apply to health information. In addition, HIPAA also contains a *Breach Notification Rule* that requires covered entities and their business associates to provide notification following a breach of unsecured PHI.

There is no nationwide data protection regulation in the US. Some regulations are limited in scope, either geographically or topic (HIPAA for health data). Data breach laws exist in each state, and all are different, making compliance a challenge.

China

The People's Republic of China has created a comprehensive cybersecurity and personal information protection framework that encompasses several laws. The most important for data privacy and protection are the Personal Information Protection Law (PIPL) and the Data Security Law (DSL), both of which came into effect in 2021. Also relevant is the Cybersecurity Law (CSL) of 2017.

The Data Security Law (DSL)[7] aims to safeguard data security and protect personal information within China. It focuses on data security and covers a broad range of data-related issues, including data processing obligations, cross-border data transfers, data localization, and cybersecurity reviews. It applies to both personal and non-personal data.

The Personal Information Protection Law (PIPL)[8] represents China's first comprehensive national-level law specifically dedicated to protecting personal information. It builds on the framework set out in the Cybersecurity Law of 2016 as well as the Data Security Law. It defines rules for the collection, use, storage, and transfer of

---

[7] For the official text (in English) see:
http://www.npc.gov.cn/englishnpc/c23934/202112/1abd8829788946ecab270e469b13c39c.shtml

[8] For the official text (in English) see: http://en.npc.gov.cn.cdurl.cn/2021-12/29/c_694559.htm

personal information by organizations. It provides specific rights to individuals regarding their personal information and imposes obligations on data controllers and processors.

While the DSL and PIPL address different aspects of data protection, they are interconnected and work together within the framework. In the remainder of this Section, we will focus on the PIPL since it provides some interesting and unique features to explore.

Understanding the spirit of the law

The purpose of the PIPL is to protect the rights and interests of individuals with regard to personal information and ensure the secure and orderly flow of personal information. The PIPL emphasizes the principle of *legality*, *legitimacy*, and *necessity* for the handling of personal information. Legitimacy is strictly defined. Penalties are serious, both for companies and for individuals who may be held responsible for violations.

Material scope

The PIPL encompasses any activity that processes (including collecting, storing, using, processing, transmitting, provisioning, and disclosing) personal information. Personal information is defined as any type of information, recorded by electronic or other means, that identifies or could identify natural persons, excluding anonymized information. This includes not only information that can identify a person on its own (like a name or identification number), but also information that can identify a person when combined with other information.

Territorial scope

The PIPL applies to the handling of personal information within the territory of the People's Republic of China. It also applies to overseas entities or individuals processing the personal information of Chinese citizens if the purpose of the processing is to provide products or services to Chinese citizens, analyze or assess the behavior of Chinese citizens, or other circumstances provided by laws and administrative regulations. This means it potentially impacts international companies, not located in China, that process the personal information of individuals in China. The extra-territorial reach of the law is very similar to the GDPR in Europe.

Requirements

Compliance with the PIPL requires adherence to the following key requirements:

1. *Legal Basis for Processing*: The PIPL requires that entities processing personal data must have a clear and legitimate purpose and can only collect data necessary for that purpose. In most cases, explicit consent is needed before personal data can be processed. However, the PIPL outlines other legal bases for processing, such as to fulfill a contract with the individual, or to respond to public health emergencies. Explicit consent is always required for processing sensitive personal data. An important difference with GDPR and other regulations is *legitimate interest* is not recognized as a legal basis for processing data.

2. *Transparency and Individual Rights*: Entities must inform individuals of the purpose, method, and scope of data processing, the retention period, and how individuals can exercise their rights under the PIPL. These rights include access to personal data, correction and deletion of inaccurate data, and withdrawal of consent. Entities must provide mechanisms to facilitate these rights.

3. *Data Minimization and Retention Limitation:* Personal data collected should be limited to what is necessary to fulfill the intended purpose and should not be retained longer than necessary.

4. *Data Security and Risk Management*: Entities are required to take appropriate measures to ensure the security of the personal data they handle. They must establish a comprehensive data governance system, including appointing a data protection officer (DPO) if processing significant amounts of personal data, implementing necessary security safeguards, conducting regular audits and risk assessments, and having a response plan for data breaches.

5. *Cross-Border Data Transfers:* If an entity wishes to transfer personal data outside of China, it must meet certain conditions, such as obtaining certification from a recognized authority, entering into a contract with the overseas recipient, or obtaining individual consent. See more below.

6. *Joint Handling*: When two or more entities jointly decide on the purpose and method of processing, they are jointly responsible for complying with the PIPL.

7. *Accountability*: Entities should implement an accountability-based governance mechanism for personal information protection, clarifying responsibilities and processes.

Rights of data subjects

The PIPL takes inspiration from GDPR in some respects. For instance, the rights of data subjects include:

- The Right to Informed Consent (must inform data subjects of the purposes, methods, and scope of information processing, and obtain their consent)

- The Right to Withdraw Consent

- The Right of Access, Rectification and Deletion

- The Right to Limit or Refuse Processing (in certain circumstances)

- The Right to Data Portability

- The Right to Object (to the handling of their personal information in specific cases)

- The Right to Lodge Complaints: Data subjects have the right to lodge complaints with the relevant competent department against personal information handlers.

Also relevant to data privacy are rights related to Automated Decision Making (such as AI systems). Under PIPL, data subjects have the right to refuse to make a decision solely based on automated decision-making, including profiling. They also have the right to request an explanation if they believe the automated decision-making process has an adverse effect.

Cross border transfers

The PIPL's requirements for cross-border data transfers are one of its most significant changes to China's data protection landscape, and it's essential that organizations understand and comply with these requirements. These clauses are specific to the PIPL. They have to meet one of the following conditions: the organization has passed a Cyberspace Administration of China (CAC) security assessment; the organization has undergone personal information protection certification conducted by a CAC-accredited agency; the organization has put in place CAC standard contractual clauses with the data recipient; or to meet compliance with laws or regulations or requirements by CAC.

The data handler shall adopt necessary measures to ensure that the foreign receiving parties' personal information handling activities comply with standards comparable to those set in the PIPL. The data handler must also inform the data subjects of the identity of the overseas recipient, the purpose and method of the processing, the types of personal information to be processed, and the ways for the individual to exercise his or her rights under Chinese law.

There is no concept of "adequacy" like there is under GDPR, which allows data transfers to certain countries that are deemed to have adequate data protection—all cross-border data transfers are treated the same. And lastly, a personal information impact assessment should be conducted.

In some cases, cross-border transfers require government approval. For certain entities, like critical information infrastructure operators or entities handling a large amount of personal data, a security assessment conducted by Chinese authorities is required for cross-border data transfers.

Enforcement

Non-compliance with PIPL can lead to hefty penalties, including fines of up to 50 million yuan or 5% of the previous year's turnover, suspension of business, revocation of business licenses, and inclusion in the Untrustworthy List.

An important clause in the PIPL is that in case of violations of the law, not only can the company be held liable, but responsible individuals (typically a CEO, DPO, or senior manager) can be held personally liable too and can face fines or sanctions.

> *The PIPL resembles the GDPR in some respects but not in others. It applies to companies that process the personal information of individuals in China or companies elsewhere processing data about Chinese citizens. Unlike GDPR, "legitimate interest" is not recognized as a legal basis for processing data. Cross-border transfers of data collected in China require informing the data subjects and, in some cases, government approval or security assessment by the Chinese Government. Another unique aspect is the possibility of personal liability of officials in a company, in case of violations of the law.*

Brazil

Brazil's *Lei Geral de Proteção de Dados* (LGPD),[9] or General Data Protection Law, went into effect on September 18, 2020. The LGPD was inspired by and is similar to the European Union's General Data Protection Regulation (GDPR). However, it also has some unique clauses.

It is worth noting that the *Marco Civil da Internet*, a Civil Rights Framework for the Internet from 2014, also has some bearing on data privacy.

---

[9] For the official text (in Portuguese) see: https://www.gov.br/mds/pt-br/acesso-a-informacao/lgpd. An English translation can be found here: https://iapp.org/resources/article/brazilian-data-protection-law-lgpd-english-translation/

Scope

The LGPD has a unique scope definition: it applies to any processing activity carried out by any person or organization, regardless of the means or country of its headquarters, provided that the processing operation is carried out in Brazil, the purpose of the activity is the offer or provision of goods or services in Brazil, or the data being processed were collected in Brazil.

The law does *not* apply to data in private or non-economic contexts if the use is exclusively for journalistic, artistic, or academic purposes, or if the data originates outside of Brazil.

This differs from GDPR, for instance, which also applies to processing EU citizen's data in countries outside the EU.

The LGPD defines "personal data" as relating to a natural person, being in either digital or non-digital form, without going into specifics about various types of personal data.

Requirements

Like the GDPR, the LGPD provides ten legal bases for processing personal data, including consent, compliance with a legal or regulatory obligation, execution of public policies, studies by research entities, execution of a contract, and legitimate interest.

Originally, the LGPD mandated the appointment of a Data Protection Officer for organizations that handle personal data in certain cases, like the GDPR. However, this clause was vetoed, and there is currently no mandatory requirement for a DPO under LGPD.

It is mandatory to adopt *privacy by default* practices when designing products or services. The LGPD also includes requirements for *data breach notifications*. In LGPD, the data controller must communicate to the national authority and to the data subject the occurrence of a security incident within a reasonable time period, while in GDPR, it explicitly states that the organization must report a data breach within seventy-two hours of its discovery. Note that Brazil has no equivalent to the EU's e-privacy directive, which makes using data for marketing purposes somewhat easier in Brazil.

Rights of data subjects

The LGPD grants data subjects several rights, including the right to confirmation of the existence of processing, access to data, correction of incomplete, inaccurate, or outdated data, anonymization, blocking or deletion of unnecessary or excessive data, data portability, deletion of personal data processed with the consent of the data subject, information about public and private entities with which the controller has shared data, and information about the possibility of denying consent and the consequences of such denial.

Consumers have been given a right under Article 9 of the LGPD to meaningful notice. This includes details like the exact reasons for data processing, the kind and duration of such processing, who is carrying out the processing and how they can be contacted, the specifics regarding data sharing with third parties, the obligations of the data-processing entity, and insights about the rights of the consumer.

Cross border transfers

Similar to GDPR, when it comes to cross-border data transfer, the LGPD has the concept of "Adequate Countries." However, at the time of writing, the Brazilian National Data Protection Authority (ANPD) has not yet determined any such countries. Another basis for cross-data transfer is specific consent given by the data subject, with prior information about the international nature of the operation.

Enforcement

The LGPD established a national authority, the National Data Protection Authority (ANPD), responsible for regulations across Brazil.

Organizations that fail to comply with the LGPD could face fines of up to 2% of their revenue in Brazil for the previous fiscal year, up to a total maximum of 50 million Brazilian Reals per violation. Other penalties include warnings, blocking or deleting personal data related to the violation, and publication of the violation after it has been duly ascertained and its occurrence has been confirmed.

The LGPD is similar to the GDPR but different in that it only applies to the processing of data carried out in Brazil, recognizes more legal bases for data processing, and does not require companies to have a DPO at the moment. Using data for marketing purposes is somewhat easier.

India

For a number of years, there was not much data privacy legislation in India. Some data protection and privacy provisions were found in other legislation and regulations, such as the *Information Technology Act, 2000* or *"The IT Act,"* along with the *Information Technology (Reasonable Security Practices and Procedures and Sensitive Personal Data or Information) Rules, 2011.* However, there was no legal framework for data protection that organizations needed to comply with. A Personal Data Protection Bill was proposed in 2019, but following a consultative process, the

Joint Parliamentary Committee withdrew it in 2022 to formulate a new comprehensive legal framework. In August 2023, a new Digital Personal Data Protection Bill (DPDPB)[10] was finally passed in parliament.

An implementation timeline has not been specified, but organizations to whom this bill will apply would be wise to start preparing. In previous years, due to the lack of regulation, companies adopted practices that relied on processing personal data without limitations and often with little safeguards. These businesses will need to significantly alter their standards, workflows, culture, and even their business models. The example of India shows that one should not always base their strategy solely on the current regulatory state but anticipate changes that are likely to come soon.

Scope

The DPDPB applies to digital information only. Section 4.1 states that the law applies to personal data collected in India, either collected from Data Principles online or offline and then digitized. It also applies if data processing "is in connection with any profiling of, or activity of offering goods or services to Data Principals within the

---

[10] See https://www.meity.gov.in/content/digital-personal-data-protection-bill-2022

territory of India." It explicitly states that the law does not apply to non-automated processing of personal data.

Exemptions

Many laws around the world provide an exemption for government entities such as law enforcement and intelligence services. The DPDPB, however, takes a rather broad definition of the conditions under which the government is exempt, causing some to express concern about possible mass surveillance. (see section 18).

Cross border transfers

Section 17, which deals with "Transfer of personal data outside India," is very short:

The Central Government may, after an assessment of such factors as it may consider necessary, notify such countries or territories outside India to which a Data Fiduciary may transfer personal data in accordance with such terms and conditions as may be specified.

On the one hand, this makes data transfers easier, as all data can be transferred to and stored in countries on the government's white-list. On the other hand, for countries that are not on the list, no transfers are possible at all.

Requirements

Most requirements are similar to GDPR:

- A lawful basis for processing is required (generally consent—either explicit consent or deemed consent). The Consent manager must register with the Indian Data Protection Board

- Appointing a Data Protection Officer (DPO) is mandatory for "Significant Data Fiduciaries"

- Data Subjects have the Right to obtain Information, Data Portability, Correction and Erasure, Grievance, Redressal, and the Right to Nominate (a representative)

- There are requirements for Data Breach notifications

- Special provisions are made for children and persons with disabilities.

But there are some differences:

- The DPDPB does not distinguish specific categories of "sensitive" data

- The DPDPB does not require Privacy by design and default.

In general, the DPDPB seems to be less stringent in terms of the requirements for data owners and processors and provides less protection to data subjects than some other regulations.

Enforcement

Interestingly, the DPDPB does not stipulate any criminal penalty for non-compliance, only financial penalties.

India is an example of a country where data privacy was largely unregulated in the past, but that has recently introduced a relatively strict law. Many nations that lack regulation so far may go through similar changes in the near future, and it is worth anticipating these developments.

Data transfers are allowed only to specific countries that the government approves, but to those countries, there are no restrictions (e.g., there is no special treatment of sensitive data). In general, the DPDPB seems to be less stringent than some other regulations.

Canada

The Office of the Privacy Commissioner of Canada enforces two federal privacy laws: the Privacy Act and the Personal Information Protection and Electronic Documents Act (PIPEDA).

The Privacy Act refers to a person's right to access and correct personal information the Canadian government holds about them. This applies to federal institutions listed under the Privacy Act Schedule of Institutions. It does not apply to political parties and political representatives.

The Personal Information Protection and Electronic Documents Act (PIPEDA) is a Canadian federal law that came into effect on January 1, 2004. The Act sets out the ground rules for how private-sector organizations collect, use, or disclose personal information in commercial activities across Canada.

PIPEDA has been established to:

1. *Establish Rules*: PIPEDA sets out rules for the management of personal information by commercial entities. It balances the individual's right to privacy with the need of organizations to collect, use, or disclose personal information for a reasonable purpose.

2. *Promote Trust*: The Act promotes consumer trust in e-commerce and includes provisions that protect electronic documents. This is crucial in today's digital age, where personal information can be shared with a simple click.

3. *Facilitate Interprovincial and International Trade*: By creating a set of uniform privacy rights, PIPEDA

facilitates trade between provinces and international partners. Having common rules helps ensure that Canadian businesses can compete globally.

PIPEDA does not apply to personal use, domestic settings, or journalistic, artistic, or literary purposes. It also does not apply to not-for-profit or charity groups and political parties. There are provincial privacy laws, specifically for the provinces of Alberta, British Columbia, and Quebec, that may be applied for these said locations instead of PIPEDA. In addition, there are also health-related privacy laws, employment-related privacy laws, and sector-specific laws applicable in certain provinces and specific cases.

The following topics under this section will now focus primarily on PIPEDA.

Material scope

PIPEDA applies to private-sector organizations that collect, use, or disclose personal information in the course of a commercial activity in Canada. This includes the selling, bartering, or leasing of donor, membership, or other fundraising lists.

In addition, PIPEDA applies to federal works, undertakings, or businesses. These are industries that are regulated by the federal government, such as airlines, banking, and broadcasting.

Territorial scope

PIPEDA applies to organizations and their commercial activities in all provinces, except those that have enacted substantially similar private-sector privacy laws, which are Quebec, British Columbia, and Alberta, as well as health information custodians in Ontario, New Brunswick, and Newfoundland and Labrador. So while we have seen cases of laws that apply nationwide (e.g., Brazil) or even regionally (EU), and the absence of (comprehensive) national laws but instead a collection of separate state laws (US), Canada has both a national law and provincial laws that supersede the national law in most respects.

Requirements

PIPEDA sets a series of requirements to protect the privacy and security of personal information in the hands of private-sector organizations. It is based on 10 Fair information principles:[11]

---

[11] https://www.priv.gc.ca/en/privacy-topics/privacy-laws-in-canada/the-personal-information-protection-and-electronic-documents-act-pipeda/p_principle/

1. *Accountability*: An organization is responsible for personal information under its control. It must appoint someone to be responsible for its compliance with these fair information principles.

2. *Identifying purposes*: The purposes for which personal information is collected should be identified by the organization before or at the time of collection.

3. *Consent*: Knowledge and consent of the individual are required for the collection, use, or disclosure of personal information. Consent must be meaningful, which means individuals must understand what they're consenting to.

4. *Limiting Collection*: The collection of personal information should be limited to that which is necessary for the identified purposes. Information should be collected by fair and lawful means.

5. *Limiting Use, Disclosure, and Retention*: Personal information should not be used or disclosed for purposes other than those for which it was collected, except with the consent of the individual or as required by law. Personal information should be retained only as long as necessary for the fulfillment of those purposes.

6. *Accuracy*: Personal information should be as accurate, complete, and up-to-date as is necessary for the purposes for which it is to be used.

7. *Safeguards*: Personal information should be protected by security safeguards appropriate to the sensitivity of the information. This includes physical measures (locked filing cabinets, restricted access to offices), technological measures (passwords, encryption), and organizational measures (security clearances, access only on a "need-to-know" basis).

8. *Openness*: An organization should make readily available to individuals specific information about its policies and practices relating to the management of personal information.

9. *Individual Access*: Upon request, an individual should be informed of the existence, use, and disclosure of his or her personal information and should be given access to that information. An individual shall be able to challenge the accuracy and completeness of the information and have it amended as appropriate.

10. *Challenging Compliance*: An individual shall be able to address a challenge concerning compliance with the above principles to the designated individual or

individuals accountable for the organization's compliance.

Rights of data subjects

Under PIPEDA, individuals (data subjects) have the following rights:

1. Right to Knowledge and Consent
2. Right to Withdraw Consent
3. Right to Access (including the right to challenge the accuracy and completeness)
4. Right to Security (of the data)
5. Right to Challenge Compliance
6. Right to be Informed of Breaches
7. Right to Data Portability

Cross border transfers

PIPEDA does not explicitly prohibit or restrict cross-border data transfers. However, organizations transferring data are considered responsible for the information in their possession, regardless of where the data is processed, and need to comply with the requirements above.

We have discussed the fact that in certain Canadian provinces, PIPEDA does not apply. However, when it comes to data transfers that cross provincial or national borders in the course of commercial activities, PIPEDA is applicable, regardless of the province the transfer emanates from.

Breach notification

Organizations are required to report to the OPC any breaches of security safeguards involving personal information under their control if it is reasonable in the circumstances to believe that the breach creates a real risk of significant harm to an individual. Organizations that knowingly fail to report a breach or to notify an individual could face fines of up to CAD $100,000.

PIPEDA applies to commercial activities in Canada, except in some provinces and some cases. Interestingly, cross-border transfers are not explicitly regulated, but the data processor remains responsible for the data and must comply with PIPEDA requirements even outside Canada.

Singapore

The Personal Data Protection Act (PDPA) was passed in 2012 by the Parliament of Singapore to govern the collection, use, and disclosure of personal data by organizations. It is a baseline law that operates across sectors, providing a consistent standard of protection for individuals while allowing organizations to harness personal data for legitimate purposes.

Scope

The PDPA applies to all organizations in Singapore, including private companies, associations, clubs, and public agencies, except where specifically exempted. It covers all personal data, defined as data from which an individual can be identified, whether true or not, and whether in electronic or other form.

PDPA does not apply to any individual acting in a personal or domestic capacity, any employee acting in the course of his or her employment with an organization, any public agency, or any business contact information.[12]

Purpose

The primary purpose of the PDPA is to protect individuals' personal data against misuse. It also seeks to enhance Singapore's competitiveness and strengthen its position as a trusted hub for businesses by ensuring a

---

[12] https://www.pdpc.gov.sg/Overview-of-PDPA/The-Legislation/Personal-Data-Protection-Act

consistent standard of data protection that will facilitate the free flow of data across jurisdictions.

Requirements

The PDPA contains the following obligations for organizations:

1. *Consent Obligation*: An organization must obtain the consent of the individual before collecting, using, or disclosing personal data for a purpose.

2. *Purpose Limitation Obligation*: An organization may collect, use, or disclose personal data about an individual only for purposes that a reasonable person would consider appropriate in the circumstances and, if applicable, have been notified to the individual.

3. *Notification Obligation*: An organization must notify individuals of the purposes for which it intends to collect, use, or disclose personal data on or before such collection, use, or disclosure of personal data.

4. *Access and Correction Obligation*: Upon request, an organization must, as soon as reasonably possible, provide an individual with his or her personal data that is in the possession or under the control of the organization and information about the ways in

which the personal data has been or may have been used or disclosed during the past year. An organization must also correct an error or omission in an individual's personal data that is in its possession or control upon the individual's request.

5. *Accuracy Obligation*: An organization must make a reasonable effort to ensure that personal data collected by or on behalf of the organization is accurate and complete if the personal data is likely to be used by the organization to make a decision that affects the individual to whom the personal data relates or disclosed by the organization to another organization.

6. *Protection Obligation*: An organization must protect personal data in its possession or under its control by making reasonable security arrangements to prevent unauthorized access, collection, use, disclosure, copying, modification, disposal, or similar risks.

7. *Retention Limitation Obligation*: An organization must cease to retain its documents containing personal data, or remove the means by which the personal data can be associated with particular individuals, as soon as it is reasonable to assume that the purpose for which that personal data was collected is no longer being served by retention of

the personal data and retention is no longer necessary for legal or business purposes.

8. *Transfer Limitation Obligation*: An organization must not transfer personal data to a country or territory outside Singapore except in accordance with the requirements prescribed under the PDPA, to ensure that organizations provide a standard of protection to personal data so transferred that is comparable to the protection under the PDPA.

9. *Accountability Obligation*: An organization must appoint one or more individuals to be responsible for ensuring that the organization complies with the PDPA. The organization must make information about its data protection policies, practices, and complaints process available on request.

Rights of data subjects

The PDPA assigns individuals the following rights:

- The Right to Consent

- The Right to Withdraw Consent

- The Right to Be Informed (the purposes for which their personal data will be collected, used, or disclosed—both at the time of collection and on request by the individual)

- The Right of Access

- The Right to Correction

- The Right to Data Portability

- The Right to Protection (from unauthorized access)

- The Right to Data Breach Notification

Breach notifications

The PDPA Amendment Bill 2020 introduced mandatory data breach notification requirements where certain thresholds are met. This provides individuals the right to be informed if their personal data has been compromised in a data breach.

Cross border transfers

Section 26 of the PDPA sets specific requirements for the transfer of personal data outside Singapore. The underlying idea is to ensure that the standard of protection afforded to personal data under the PDPA is not undermined when that data is transferred outside Singapore. The requirements consist of the *Transfer Limitation Obligation* (The data must retain protection similar to PDPA when it is transferred outside of Singapore); *Due Diligence* and *Legally Enforceable Obligations* (such as contractual obligations, statutory obligations; binding corporate rules; or other legally binding instruments).

Exceptions to the data transfer limitations exist. Most importantly, if the individual has consented to the transfer of personal data after being informed of the possible risks, the data may be transferred without ensuring a comparable standard of protection.

Enforcement

Failing to comply with PDPA can result in penalties, including Financial Penalties, Prosecution (of individuals), and Civil Actions, and the organization will likely be ordered to stop the collection, use, or disclosure of personal data and to destroy personal data collected in contravention of the Act.

Singapore's PDPA is a comprehensive regulation with the usual requirements for consent, purpose limitation, accuracy, protection, and data breach notifications. It also has a requirement for accountability, which means appointing staff to ensure compliance and sharing internal data privacy policies on request.

There are limitations on cross-border data transfers that imply that the protection of the data must not be reduced when the data is transferred to another country. However, there is a way around this by asking individuals for explicit consent after being informed of possible risks.

South Africa

The Protection of Personal Information Act (popularly known as POPIA) is a South African law that regulates the processing of personal information by both public and private organizations. The Act was passed in 2013 and took effect on July 1, 2020.

The purpose of POPIA is to protect the privacy of individuals and to give them control over their personal information. It also aims to standardize compliance in line with international standards, aligning closely with regulations such as the GDPR.

Scope

POPIA applies to all organizations that process any personal information in South Africa. The Act also applies to organizations that process personal information of South African citizens or residents, even if these organizations are not located in South Africa and the data is processed elsewhere. Exceptions exist for national security, law enforcement, or scientific research.

The POPI Act includes specific provisions about direct marketing, automated decision making, and the processing of special personal information such as religious or philosophical beliefs, race or ethnic origin, trade union membership, political persuasion, health, sexual life, or criminal behavior.

Interestingly, POPIA not only applies to natural persons, but also to existing legal persons such as companies. This differs from most other regulations (including GDPR) that only apply to natural persons.

Requirements

The POPI Act outlines several key requirements for the responsible parties (those who determine the purpose and means for processing personal information):

- *Accountability*: The responsible party is accountable for the lawful processing of personal information.

- *Processing Limitation*: Personal information must be processed in a reasonable manner that does not infringe on the privacy of the data subject. It should be appropriate, relevant, and not excessive.

- *Purpose Specification*: Personal information should be collected for a specific, explicitly defined, and lawful purpose related to a function or activity of the responsible party.

- *Further Processing Limitation*: Further processing of personal information must be compatible with the purpose for which it was initially collected.

- *Information Quality:* The responsible party must ensure that the personal information is complete, accurate, not misleading, and updated where necessary.

- *Openness*: The responsible party must ensure transparency with the data subject regarding the collection, nature of the information, purpose of collection, and existence of the right to object to the processing.

- *Security Safeguards*: The responsible party is required to secure the integrity and confidentiality of personal information by taking appropriate measures to prevent loss, damage, or unlawful access to personal information.

- *Data Subject Participation*: The data subject has the right to access and correct their personal information.

Rights of data subjects

POPIA grants a number of rights to data subjects that are similar to GDPR:

- The Right to be Notified

- The Right of Access

- The Right to Correction or Deletion

- The Right to Object

- The Right to Complain

- Right to be Informed

- Right to be Informed of Security Compromises (i.e. Data Breaches)

However, it also adds some unique elements:

- The Right to *Prevent Direct Marketing*: POPIA gives data subjects the right to refuse direct marketing communications. Entities need to obtain consent before they can send marketing communications.

- Right to *Prevent Automated Decision Making*: Data subjects also have the right to not be subject to a decision that is based solely on the automated processing of personal information intended to provide a profile of such person, such as their performance at work, creditworthiness, health, personal preferences, etc.

Cross border transfers

Section 72 of the POPIA speaks to cross-border data transfers. It states that data transfers to other countries are allowed if:

- These countries offer Adequate legal protection

- The data subject has consented to the transfer of its personal information

- It is necessary for the performance of a contract (in some cases)

- The transfer is in the interests of the data subject (in some cases)

- The transfer is for the benefit of the data subject (in some cases)

In other words, any organization wishing to transfer personal information outside South Africa needs to ensure that the country to which the data is being sent has similar protections to POPIA or that the data subject has consented to the transfer or qualifies for one of the other conditions. These options make the regulation much less strict than GDPR or some other regulations.

At the same time, the fact that the POPIA applies to companies as well creates complications when transferring data about companies outside South Africa. Most countries would not qualify as "adequate" according to option (a) because their data privacy regulations do not apply to companies. This is something organizations need to be well aware of.

Enforcement

The Information Regulator is the independent body responsible for enforcing POPIA. The powers of the Regulator include investigating complaints, issuing compliance notices, and imposing sanctions. Organizations that fail to comply with POPIA may be subject to several sanctions, including fines of up to 10 million South African rand (ZAR).

Key takeaways

The POPI Act applies to operations in South Africa or South African citizens' data processed elsewhere. It broadly follows the GDPR model, but its definition of Scope is unique, with provisions about direct marketing, automated decision making, and specific types of personal data. Cross-border transfer limitations are significantly less stringent than in GPDR. Although data about companies is tricky, the POPIA applies to such data as well.

Comparing privacy regulations

We have seen a wide variety of regulations. On the one hand, we have seen GDPR, which is very comprehensive and strict on data transfers. On the other hand, we have seen India, which does not have a specific data protection law at the moment (but that does not mean organizations should not be prepared for regulation of data in India in the future). We have seen the US, where regulation is sparse and fragmented. We have seen Brazil's law, which is inspired by the GDPR but with specific changes to meet the needs of the country. We have seen the People's Republic of China, which has an integrated framework of laws for data security, personal information, and other topics. We have seen Singapore that tries to strike a balance between protecting its citizens' data and making the country attractive and competitive for businesses.

Governments realize that, increasingly, the character of business and data is globalizing and that the diversity of regulations in the world is hampering data flows in organizations. Several countries have purposely revised their regulations to be more in line with GDPR, as a "gold standard" that will satisfy many other nations as a sufficient guarantee that data transferred to this nation will be safe.

An interesting aspect of regulations is their extraterritorial reach. In other words, does the regulation apply to entities outside the country? Almost all regulations do apply outside the borders of the country if the data pertains to citizens of the country. So, even if cross-border data transfers are permitted, receiving entities may still need to comply with the regulations of the originating country of the data.

Let's compare a few key aspects of these regulations:

	Territorial Scope	Material Scope	Require-ments	Cross-Border Xfer Limitations
Brazil	national	medium	strict	medium
Canada	national (with exceptions)	broad	medium	medium
China	national	broad	strict	strict
EU	regional	broad	strict	strict
India (as of 2023)	-	-	none	low
South Africa	national	broad	medium	low
Singapore	national	broad	medium	medium
US	fragmented	narrow	strict	low

CHAPTER 4

The Challenges of Data Privacy in Multinational Organizations

I n the previous chapter, we have seen the diversity of existing regional, national, and sub-national regulations. Organizations operating globally handle data that flow across various countries and jurisdictions. In this chapter, we will discuss the key challenges these organizations face and the impact on their data privacy strategies.

We speak about a data privacy strategy rather than a compliance strategy because we think your strategy should not only be focused on compliance. Risk mitigation is also an objective, as notifications after a data breach can be very costly. Cultural and ethical aspects also play a role. Customers pay a lot of attention to the corporate values of a company, and bad behavior in terms of data privacy can erode public trust or cause reputational damage.

Organizational data flows

In today's digitalized world, data can often move across geographical boundaries without us knowing, and transmitting personal data across national borders means various regulations apply in countries that the data moves through.

Non-compliance with these laws can lead to significant financial penalties and reputational damage.

A detailed data flow map is needed to identify where data originates, where it is processed, where it is stored, and how it moves within and beyond the organization. Of course, understanding your global data flow is a good data governance practice in general. It is a requirement for establishing robust security measures. Data moving across borders may become susceptible to breaches and other cyber threats. Organizations can better anticipate vulnerabilities and mitigate potential risks by having a clear picture of these flows.

One important concept that can complement the work of dataflows is the data lifecycle. The data lifecycle refers to the different phases that data goes through, from collection, use, retention, and disclosure to deletion. The lifecycle serves as an end-to-end framework for how data is processed through an organization. Each phase requires different approaches to data privacy implementation.

When creating dataflows, it is important to know how data is being used and by whom at various stages.

However, even if creating dataflows is a well-recognized good practice for data governance, it does not mean organizations necessarily have that all under control. In large organizations, data has been collected or processed in different departments and corners for many decades as part of their daily operations. Only recently, the realization that data is a valuable corporate asset and the need to comply with data protection laws have made the organization start data governance programs. Most of these programs have yet to reach the stage where they have clear insight into global data flows.

The rapid digitization of society means that many organizations are going through some form of digital transformation. This process, spanning over several years, is integral to leveraging the full potential of modern technology in the corporate landscape. Part of this transformation is the optimization of data exchange within the organization. This typically involves dismantling data silos to facilitate seamless information flow across various departments. In fact, some forward-thinking entities take this a step further, restructuring their operational model to become entirely data-driven.

To achieve this, organizations typically formulate a data strategy. This strategy outlines the various data sources and the organization's diverse data needs. The strategic plan will often incorporate the consolidation of data into a central repository. This could be a data warehouse, data lake, or another centralized data structure, with the aim of making data more accessible and actionable across the organization.

However, this can quickly cause tension with data privacy objectives – either the organization's internal policies or external compliance requirements. The problem is that data strategies tend to emphasize an efficiency and usability perspective. Its aim is to make informed decisions based on available data. Therefore, the focus tends to be on data sharing and how it can be made available for use. Data strategies need to be looked at from a data privacy perspective as well.

To comply with data privacy regulations, the easiest solution would be to keep all data in the place (country or region) where it is collected and never move it or use it elsewhere. For some data, that may be possible. For other data that is clearly not desirable, analyzing it across the organization is imperative. Thus, the data privacy strategy and the data strategy can sometimes have contrary objectives. One needs to find a balance between the two. Organizations should develop a data strategy based on a framework[13] covering data defense and offense

---

[13]https://hbr.org/2017/05/whats-your-data-strategy

approaches. The data offensive activities focus on customer business functions, while data defense activities focus on minimizing risks and ensuring compliance with regulations. The data privacy strategy could feed into or be part of the overall data strategy from the defense perspective. At a minimum, there should be alignment between the data privacy strategy and the overall data strategy.

Cross-border data transfers

Cross-border data transfers are a critical part of multinational companies' operations, given their global nature and the need for seamless information sharing across the globe. However, complying with various national regulations can pose significant challenges. As we have seen in Chapter 3, the legal and regulatory landscape for data privacy and protection varies greatly from country to country. It is a best practice to meet the most stringent legal requirements of the countries that one works with in terms of cross-border transfers. However, it is also important to understand the implications and risks involved to the organization in working with countries that do not have adequate privacy laws.

As we have seen, regulations around the world can differ in anything from the definition of "personal data" to the recognition of different roles in collecting, controlling, processing, or using data, to the definition of who are considered the data subjects that the law protects (citizens of the country or legal residents or even companies, in the case of South Africa). That makes defining a corporate policy extra hard since even basic definitions need to be fluid and dependent on the (geographical) context of the data.

The inconsistency between different national regulations can create dilemmas for multinational companies. A practice that is acceptable in one country might be illegal in another. For instance, data localization laws in countries like Russia and China require certain data to be stored within their borders, which can conflict with regulations in other countries or make it difficult to centralize data management.

However, as we will see in Chapter 5, the variations in global data privacy regulations can also be taken advantage of in a data privacy strategy.

Legal and regulatory challenges

Global organizations often grapple with the complexities of disparate legal and regulatory landscapes. Given that each jurisdiction might have its unique set of data protection laws, understanding and complying with each can pose a significant challenge. Furthermore, some jurisdictions, such as the European Union's General Data Protection Regulation (GDPR), have extraterritorial applicability clauses in their privacy laws, making the challenge even more multifaceted.

Consider, for example, a European company with a subsidiary in Brazil. While processing the personal data of EU citizens, it must comply with the GDPR. Simultaneously, the data of its customers that is being processed in Brazil would be subject to Brazil's privacy laws, such as the LGPD), which have different provisions and requirements. This divergence in legal obligations can sometimes result in conflicts of laws, leading to a predicament for organizations in reconciling these conflicting requirements.

In addition to the challenge of conflicting laws, organizations must also stay abreast of changes in regulations across the different jurisdictions they operate in. Changes in privacy laws can necessitate adjustments in data handling practices, requiring agility and constant vigilance on the part of the organizations.

It is also important to highlight that there are also legal and regulatory considerations in the use of Privacy Enhancing Technologies, which are technologies that provide capabilities for sharing and processing sensitive data. These technologies must be used in alignment with existing laws and policies and will require legal experts' guidance on its application. Different laws and jurisdictions may have issues or concerns about the adequacy of technologies' solutions for specific projects or contexts.

Lack of clarity

Some regulations are very clear and/or have substantial jurisprudence that one can rely upon. Other regulations leave a lot of questions. For instance, the (now abolished) PDPB in India.

Unlike the GDPR, the PDPB places heightened restrictions on transfers of personal data outside India. The PDPB does not explicitly set forth requirements for transfers of personal data. However, it prohibits the transfer of "critical personal data," which has yet to be defined by the government, except in certain circumstances. For example, data fiduciaries may transfer such data where necessary to provide prompt health or emergency services or where permitted by the government and the DPA.

Contractual obligations with third parties

Multinational companies often engage third-party vendors for data processing activities. These vendors may be spread across the globe, and ensuring they comply with various national regulations is a significant task. This may require drafting complex contracts and continuous monitoring of their practices. These contracts must include clear expectations and documentation of data management and handling, including details on the access, processing, sharing, retention, and destruction of the data. Organizations should periodically and when needed, perform audits on the vendors to ensure compliance.

Data breach

Moving data across borders also increases the *risk of a data breach* due to the involvement of various networks, systems, and parties. Complying with breach notification laws, which vary by country, can be challenging and costly. Notifying affected parties in compliance with diverse jurisdictions can be a logistical and legal challenge.

Cultural and ethical considerations

Legal and regulatory challenges are just part of the equation. Global organizations must also grapple with cultural and ethical considerations.

A good understanding of local cultural sensitivities is required for any international organization as it can help adapt products or services to local markets more effectively. But there are specific implications for data privacy, too. The interpretation and importance of privacy can significantly vary across cultures. While some societies might highly emphasize individual privacy, others might prioritize communal or societal benefits over individual privacy rights. One study[14] that examined participants from eight countries, Canada, China, Germany, the United States, the United Kingdom, Sweden, Australia, and India, developed and presented a cross-cultural prediction model on privacy that includes cultural, demographic, attitudinal, and contextual predictors. It highlights the difference between the viewpoints on privacy of individualistic countries versus collectivistic countries.

In navigating these cultural differences, organizations must balance respecting privacy rights and achieving their business objectives. This balance might look different in various cultural contexts. Hence, a one-size-fits-all approach to privacy may not be feasible or desirable.

One objective is to act ethically. For a company or organization to be recognized as having strong ethical principles, doing "the right thing" will benefit its business objectives or mission.

A related objective is building trust with your customers or audience. Trust and transparency are critical to business

---

[14] https://petsymposium.org/popets/2017/popets-2017-0019.php

success. Organizations can contribute to this by being clear and open about their data handling practices and by giving individuals control over their data. This can go a long way in building a strong customer relationship and maintaining a brand reputation globally. And it is not just customers—being sensitive to local cultures fosters better relationships with local partners, suppliers, and government authorities.

For example, data minimization is a requirement in many regulations. But it is also a good way to build trust. Categorize the data you intend to collect into essential, nice-to-have, and optional. Check the nice-to-have and optional data against local values to determine whether people might take issue with a particular data element. Avoid collecting controversial data that is not essential.

Another good practice is transparency. Be clear and upfront about what data you are collecting and for what purpose. Explain this in as plain language as possible and not in an intentionally small font!

The complexities and disparity in international data privacy regulations represent challenges for any global organization. It requires a clear understanding of multinational data flows, awareness of the legal and regulatory landscape, and a nuanced appreciation of cultural and ethical considerations.

In the next chapter, we will use the aspects identified here to create a data privacy and protection strategy. We will explore practical tools and frameworks, such as privacy by design and data protection impact assessments, which can help organizations maintain a robust, compliant, and ethical data protection posture.

CHAPTER 5

Creating a Strategy

When when we build a data privacy strategy, it should not only be viewed through a compliance lens. Based on a study[15] published by Cisco in 2020, for every dollar spent on privacy, the average organization is getting $2.70 in associated benefits. In addition, the study also states that organizations received significant business benefits from privacy beyond compliance, which include better agility and innovation, increased competitive advantage, improved attractiveness to investors, and greater customer trust.

This means that we need to align with the organization's overall business strategy when developing a data privacy strategy. In other words, the data privacy initiatives should be presented as enablers to meet the organization's objectives and not only be viewed as a compliance activity.

A good starting point is ensuring that the data privacy strategy is part of the data strategy of the organization. A

---

[15] Cisco 2020 Data Benchmark Study

data strategy encompasses data governance, data management, data security, technology tools and infrastructure, and change management. If data privacy is considered within all these strategic and technical areas, it will help the organization maximize the benefits of implementing privacy.

One possible route to take is a risk-based approach. This starts by considering that every piece of PII that you own is a risk, and you need to weigh that risk with the benefits for the business. Some data may be necessary: you cannot process online orders for garden furniture without storing the address of the recipient. Some data may be nice-to-have, and you may discover that some data you collected is not used or useful. The engineers, business analysts, and the marketing department in your organization will all likely want to keep as much data for as long as possible – you never know when it comes in handy! But this is often not allowed by law and not wise from a risk management perspective.

It is also good to keep in mind the important relation to IT Security. The physical and electronic protection of the data greatly affects the risk of data privacy incidents.

Certain roles in your organization will be important stakeholders in the data privacy strategy that will be key in defining the priorities, providing the requirements and limitations, and implementing the strategy. The Chief

Information Officer (CIO), Chief Data Officer (CDO), heads of marketing, operations of IT infrastructure, and the Chief Information Security Officer (CISO) are key partners, and therefore important to engage them throughout the process of developing a strategy.

The strategy design process

The process we recommend to develop a strategy for data privacy contains seven steps:

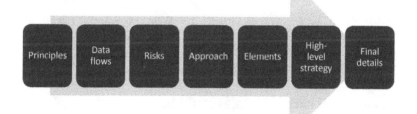

1. Establish principles

2. Analyze major data flows

3. Assess risks in current major data flows (local risks and data transfer risks)

4. Decide on a high-level approach with senior management and other stakeholders

5. Analyze your possible elements for a data privacy strategy

6. Decide on a high-level strategy and review with stakeholders

7. Work out the details

We will now go through these steps in detail.

Establish principles

To have a solid basis for decision making in designing a data privacy strategy, it is useful to start with mapping out some principles. Which values are non-negotiable for your organization? If your organization already has a set of core values, how do they relate to data?

Examples of such principles could be:

- Act with integrity to customers

- Be transparent, fair, and truthful to our customers

- Be a trustworthy company

- Cultivate a culture of respect, internally and to our business partners

- Be culturally sensitive and altruistic

- Operate ethically

- Promote accountability in the organization

This also provides a starting point in developing your organization's privacy vision and mission statements. These are short statements that define the vision and goals of the privacy function in the organization while aligning with the overall organization's objectives.

Basing your data privacy strategy on your corporate principles will help you at times when a decision needs to be made between the benefits and risks of the processing of certain data. They will also help you get buy-in from senior management and others for the data privacy strategy.

At the technical level, there are principles that one can derive from best practices in data protection. These include:

- Avoid over-collection. Do a review of whether all information collected is actually used. Do not collect information you do not need, and dispose of information at the earliest moment. Every piece of information you retain carries a cost and constitutes a risk.

- Keep data in place as much as possible. Moving not only increases data privacy compliance issues but also introduces security risks.

- Keep track of what data you collect.

- Be transparent to the data subjects.

- Ensure that data is accurate and kept up to date.

- Apply appropriate security safeguards to protect data.

These technical principles will help form a basis for the blueprint of your strategy. Rather than fixing problems once they arise, these principles prevent problems from happening in the first place.

Analyze major data flows

Much of your time will be dedicated to analyzing the major data flows in your organization. In Chapter 4, we already spoke about data flows and creating a detailed data flow map. Depending on the size of your company, this can take weeks, months, or even years. You may need to talk to data owners, IT staff, and staff in offices in each country your organization operates in. If your organization already has solid data governance mechanisms, you will have a head start. If your industry is subject to specific regulations, some of this analysis may already have been done to comply with regulatory requirements. But even then, these maps of data are likely far from complete for the purposes of data privacy.

Imagine you are an e-commerce company in the US, with a fulfillment team working remotely from Brazil, serving a customer in Europe and shipping products to them directly from your factory in China. It is a tall order to keep track of every piece of customer data collected and shared with colleagues in another country or with a third party. Most companies do not have that clarity. Yet, this is exactly what you need when designing a data privacy strategy.

Setting the ambition level

When you start analyzing the data flows in your company, you may want to get a high-level picture of the complexity of the situation. You want to compare that to the available resources (how large is your team?), the level of cooperation you can expect throughout the organization, and the required timeframe. There is no point in setting ambitious goals that are not achievable.

Determine a realistic level of expectation in your organization. This might be one of the following:

Maturity level	Characteristics
1. Bare minimum	Awareness of personal data that is being shared externally or moved across borders.
2. Minimum	Awareness of personal data being collected, stored, processed, used, shared, or moved.

Maturity level	Characteristics
3. Better	Awareness of all personal data and other sensitive data being collected, created, stored, processed, used, shared, or moved.
4. Optimal	Full awareness of all data flows in the company, whether personal, sensitive, or other data being collected, created, stored, processed, used, shared, or moved.

Once you have determined the realistic maturity level, you will want to check with senior management whether this can be agreed upon as the objective, at least for the time being. Otherwise, some parameters, such as resources or timeframe, must change.

Data inventory

Having established the maturity level you aim for, the next step would be to do an initial stock of the data collected in each location where you do operations. Location here may mean country, division, or branch. You will also need to collect the necessary metadata, including the type of data, where it is collected (e.g., the country), how it is collected (the context), how it is stored, any consent that was obtained before collecting the data, and retention policies. Depending on your field of business, there may be other metadata you will want to collect, such as this example of a data element:

Customer Address

Type	Where coll.	How coll.	Retention	Consent	Sensitive	Storage
Text	Europe	User input (order form)	Indefinitely	Implicit	No	CM SQL db (Germany, EU)

Even within one country, which part of your organization collects the data may be relevant because it may have been collected for a specific purpose and/or consent may have been obtained for a specific purpose or context. The customer support department may have collected data to help a customer with a problem they have with a product. The marketing department may have other uses for the records collected in this process, which may not be a valid purpose.

You might obtain this information by looking at database schemas, process flows, or the documentation of applications. Likely, it will be a combination. Of course, you are looking here for personal data, not all data in the company. But as we have seen in Chapter 2, personal data can take many forms and includes all data that can somehow be tied back to a particular individual.

Cookies are an interesting form of data collection in that you, as an organization, can create them and are the only one with access. Still, you do not hold the information— the data subjects themselves do, perhaps unknowingly, as the data collected resides in their Internet browser. This can make things easier for you (no wonder cookies are so popular), but it still means you are bound by the rules you specified in the privacy notice to the users. It is important to be transparent with the users on collecting and processing their personal data.

Mapping data movements

The next challenge is looking at the data flows. Again, process flows and the documentation of applications will be sources of information. Interviews with staff involved in the processing of information can be particularly helpful, but they cannot be the only source. Often, organizations collect and store data that no one is aware of and that is not being used. These unnecessary risk exposures should be eliminated.

Documenting these movements in a way they can be visualized and studied can be challenging. For simple examples, a spreadsheet or flowchart may suffice. But as the number of data elements grows, this can quickly become overwhelming, even chaotic. You will want to use a database to store your data flows and queries to study them. Some may even want to use a knowledge graph, a type of database that is particularly good at storing connections between data. Your database should be able to answer queries you may have, for instance, *"What are sensitive data collected from customers in the UK?"* or *"What data elements are moved from the EU to our data processing team in India?"* and ideally have some tools to visualize this information.

The data lifecycle

In the previous chapter, we spoke briefly about the data lifecycle. This is another useful model to get insight into how data is being used. The way you store the information you have collected about data elements in a database or other form will ideally also give you a way of visualizing the data lifecycle of each element. This is particularly useful in determining the risk associated with each data element in the next step.

Assess risks

Now that you have a clearer idea of the data flows in your organization, you are ready to assess your organization's risk exposure. Issues when working with data can occur throughout the data lifecycle and are caused by the lack of organizational and technical safeguards. The risks in collecting and processing data include:

- Violation of regulations in the collection of data (e.g., if it is done without a legal basis)

- Violation of regulations in the processing of data (e.g., if data is used for a different purpose than was originally specified)

- Violation of regulations in cross-border data transfers

- Data breaches (the cost of informing authorities and data subjects and the reputation harm done)

- Social and cultural backlash, even if your data collection and processing is within the law (e.g., the excessive individualization of user experience or individual targeting in marketing campaigns may backfire)

Decide on a high-level approach

Analyzing data elements, data flows, and risk exposure gives you a good idea of your challenges. It is time to formulate a high-level approach. This does not need to be a large document—it could be written in one page, even one paragraph, if needed. But in most cases, you will want to explain your reasoning and clarify what this approach means because you will need to ensure all stakeholders are on board. The high-level approach describes what framework or model will be the basis for your strategy. There are several standard frameworks to choose from to determine your approach. Here are some possible choices:

Principles-based approach

Implementing a global privacy framework based on common principles is a good option if your organization already has a set of principles to which it is strongly committed. Other examples of principles-based approaches are the OECD Guidelines,[16] the Asia-Pacific Economic Cooperation (APEC) Privacy Framework,[17] and the UN's data privacy policy, which is based on the UN System's data privacy principles.[18]

Ethics-centered approach

Somewhat related to the previous option, the ethics-centered approach goes beyond the need for compliance with regulation and puts ethics at the center of your approach. Research institutions and universities may well choose this approach. Yet also, a number of technology startups have embraced this approach, especially those in emerging fields like AI and biotech, that explore new boundaries and, therefore, new ethical dilemmas that society has no easy answers for.

---

[16] See: https://doi.org/10.1787/9789264196391-en

[17] See: https://www.apec.org/Publications/2017/08/APEC-Privacy-Framework-(2015)

[18] See: https://unsceb.org/privacy-principles

Risk-based approach

Adopting a risk-based approach is a good option for companies that aim to mitigate financial, legal, and reputational risks related to data privacy. This means the strategy will likely be structured to contain (continuous) assessments, controls, policies, and procedures to mitigate identified risks and regular reviews, so the controls remain effective and relevant.

Standards-based approach

Adopting international standards and frameworks can be useful for organizations in strongly regulated industries or environments, such as banks, healthcare providers, or government agencies.

One example of an international standard is ISO/IEC 27701.[19] In the United States, the National Institute of Standards and Technology (NIST) publishes many frameworks and standards, including the NIST Privacy Framework.[20] Some of these frameworks go beyond data privacy and can be helpful to align, for instance, with cybersecurity risk management.

---

[19] See: https://www.iso.org/standard/71670.html

[20] See: https://www.nist.gov/privacy-framework

Technology-driven approach

This approach puts technology at the center of achieving data privacy objectives. There are many solutions, such as Privacy Enhancing Technologies (PETs), to automatically enforce certain privacy controls. There are also automated tools for data mapping, risk assessment, and consent management to ensure consistent application of privacy measures. This approach might be preferred in a highly digital environment where managing the digital infrastructure is paramount, where large volumes of data are being handled, or where the business environment is highly volatile.

Given the priorities of the top leadership in your organization, the objectives of data privacy, the culture of your organization, and the principles, values, frameworks, and strategies already in place, you must determine which approach will work best. You are, of course, not restricted to the options mentioned above. You can formulate your own approach and combine elements of various approaches. It is important to realize that the high-level approach will not be a turn-key recipe for your organization and that, especially in different regions, it must be adapted to specific legislations and cultures. Organizational realities also pay a role. It is common for large organizations to have regional offices with a large degree of independence and their own "culture." The North American office may not want to take the same approach to privacy as the European office, even when interpreting and responding to the same regulation like GDPR. It may thus not be possible to have one global privacy standard for the organization, as much as that would make sense strategically.

Analyze your possible elements

You have already done a significant amount of preparatory work for your strategy. We recommend another preparatory step before starting to structure it and write down the strategy.

We want to create a check-list of high-level issues that we must address in our strategy. Examples of such issues are:

- *Data minimization* (collection, storage, retention, movement. Consider data minimization as a fundamental principle in your strategy, as it is required by many regulations.)

- *Data processing* (What can be analyzed now? What do we need in its raw form? Would it do to create synthetic data based on the data collected and move that synthetic data instead?)

- *Geographic strategy* (Where to store and process which data? How to minimize movement?)

- *Technology strategy* (How can technology such as PETs and electronic data governance solutions be leveraged?)

While studying the data flows in your organization and identifying needs and risks, in your conversations with various stakeholders, and while deciding on a high-level approach, you have probably encountered other issues that you realized need addressing in the strategy. Focus on high-level topics and not detailed issues. Instead, keep detailed issues on the list to return to during the implementation phase.

Here are some more examples of topics that you may want to include:

- *Continuous Improvement and Agility* (Privacy landscapes are constantly changing, both in terms of threats and regulations. A strategy and the governance mechanisms and controls should not be static but should include regular reviews, audits, and feedback mechanisms and have the agility to be updated and refined when needed.)

- *Stakeholder Collaboration* (Collaborating with other business units, legal teams, IT departments, and external stakeholders is essential to ensure that the privacy strategy is holistic and robust. What mechanisms will be put in place to enable this collaboration?)

- *Culture* (Foster a privacy-aware culture throughout the organization)

- *Transparency and Accountability* (Be transparent to stakeholders, especially data subjects. Implement mechanisms to demonstrate accountability, such as DPIAs, audits, and documenting data processing activities).

- *Incident Preparedness and Response* (No matter how well organized we are, incidents will happen. Develop a robust incident response plan to address incidents such as data breaches).

Decide on a high-level strategy

It is now time to write an outline for your strategy. In the preparatory work done in the previous steps of the process, you have already collected all the essential elements. What do we need to do to structure them into a coherent strategy?

No one model fits all, and it is impossible to give you a standard outline for a data privacy strategy. We can provide this template as a starting point:

1. Executive Summary
2. Introduction
   - Background on the organization.

- Importance of data privacy for the organization.

3. Objectives and Goals
- Organization's privacy vision and/or mission statements

4. Principles and Values
- Values of the organization
- Transparency and communication with stakeholders
- Other commitments

5. Organizational Structures and Roles
- Designation of Data Privacy Officer (DPO) or equivalent role
- Boards or committees
- Roles and responsibilities of key stakeholders

6. Regulatory Landscape
- Review of relevant data privacy regulations and standards that the organization needs to comply with in various countries and business

7. Policies and Procedures
- Development and maintenance of data privacy policies
- Consent management
- Management of data subject requests
- Incident preparedness and response
  - Data breach response plan

- ■ Regular testing of incident response mechanisms
- Guidelines for specific data processing activities
- Guidelines for application development

8. Data Landscape
- A high-level mapping of data flows in the organization

9. Risk Assessment
- Identified data privacy risks and potential impact
- Third-party risks—privacy considerations in vendor agreements and contracts
- Prioritization of risks
- Alignment with IT risk management

10. Data Processing Strategy
- Data flow optimization
- Data minimization
- Data processing tools

11. Data Governance
- Alignment with current data governance practices
- Additional data governance needs

12. Technology Strategy
- Tools for data governance and data management
- Privacy enhancing Tools

- Alignment with IT infrastructure management

13. Cultural Change Management
    - Foster a privacy-aware culture
    - Awareness and data literacy for all staff

14. Monitoring and Compliance
    - Internal audits and privacy impact assessments
    - Mechanisms to ensure regulatory compliance
    - Key performance indicators to measure the effectiveness of the privacy program

15. Continuous Improvement and Adaptation
    - Feedback loops
    - Mechanisms for updating the privacy strategy based on feedback, changes in regulations, changes in data use at the organization, and technological advancements.

While it is not a separate step in our process, you must discuss the outline of the strategy with relevant stakeholders. These include senior management, the legal department, the IT department (in particular IT security, but also infrastructure and application development), data owners or stewards, and major data users—those whose work depends on data and who will be affected day-to-day by the data privacy measures put in place.

Work out the details

Now that we have the outline and hopefully have obtained an agreement with all stakeholders on what the data privacy strategy will look like, we can start filling in the details. Many of the headings in our outline still require significant study and analysis.

We will not go through each of the chapter headings of the strategy template—some are obvious, and some have already been addressed in previous chapters, such as the regulatory landscape. But we will highlight a few areas.

Risk Assessment

We recommend that you consider a number of aspects in turn. You can do so for each data element or group of data elements with similar characteristics.

Collection

How risky is the data that is collected? Sensitive data, as defined in the country where it is collected, may require special treatment. Some data about ethnicity, religion, or health conditions may be particularly controversial in certain countries or among certain groups.

Data transfers

Some transfers between certain countries may be easy— either because the originating country does not regulate data transfers or because the destination country is recognized as providing "adequate" protection, and, therefore, the transfer is allowed. Other transfers can be difficult or controversial—you may be clearly violating the law, or the status may be unclear in some cases. Those are risks that your organization may or may not be willing to take. It is also important to realize that any data transfer, even within one country or office, represents an IT security risk. The safest approach is never moving the data, but this is not a practical recommendation in many cases.

Processing

Some forms of processing of the data are clearly within the legitimate use that it was intended for—in terms of regulations, you have a "legal basis" to do so. Some uses may be clear violations of the law and/or betrayals of the trust of your customers. But other cases will be somewhere in between, and it is your job to determine the slippery slope you are on when processing data in a certain way. This is where working with data owners and legal teams to determine whether the processing meets legal basis would be useful.

Storage

This is partly an IT operations and IT Security question. Different types of storage, such as onsite or in the cloud and self-managed or managed by a 3rd party, come with different levels of risk.

This also relates to retention. For instance, some companies keep customers' credit card numbers on file to make future purchases even more frictionless. Some companies will not store any such data out of principle to reduce the risk and impact of data breaches that might happen in the future.

You should document your evaluations depending on the ambition level of your study. At the very least, we recommend a high-medium-low scale and a special "Alert" indication for situations that require immediate action. Spending on the scope of your research, you may likely want to store the risk assessments in a spreadsheet or database, and ideally have some ways to visualize the reports. Here are some examples of what such visuals might look like.

Situation	Example	Risk
For data elements	Customer address	High
For data transfers	Transferring customer address from one internal office to another	High (GDPR data transfer violation)
For data processing	Extracting postal codes from addresses to perform market analysis	Low
For data storage	Storing addresses indefinitely in a relational database	Medium (Database contains personal data and is open for remote access with authentication)

It is also important to align privacy risk management efforts with an organization's wider enterprise risk management framework. For instance, the company's relationship between PII and other sensitive data needs protection and careful handling. A comprehensive strategy might as well incorporate both.

Technology Strategy

Two big categories of tools are relevant to a data privacy strategy: data governance tools and Privacy Enhancing Technologies (PETs).

Data governance tools start with a data catalog: a master database of all data in the organization. Depending on the level of data maturity, your organization may already have one. Otherwise, that process needs to be started but kept separate from the data privacy strategy, since creating a data catalog is a huge effort in itself. Even if a data catalog already exists, you may want to check if all the metadata you need for data privacy is indeed documented.

Other data governance tools focus on data lineage, data quality, metadata management, master data management, lifecycle management, policy management, and audit and compliance. We don't mean to say that all of these are required to implement your data privacy strategy. They are certainly not. But they can all be helpful in various respects. Often, these are functionalities on a larger platform for data governance.

Privacy Enhancing Technologies are smaller, tactical tools. Some, like forms of Data Masking, might be found as functionalities in larger platforms, but since a number of them are quite new, they likely haven't found their way yet into enterprise products. The main categories here are anonymization/pseudonymization, encryption, differential privacy, and synthetic data. These techniques can support various objectives in your data privacy strategy, including data minimization and managing access control.

Pseudonymization replaces identifying fields within a dataset with artificial identifiers or pseudonyms so the dataset is not directly associated with an individual. However, since linkages between the original identifier and the pseudonym remain, the original data can be restored and re-identified. Anonymization removes or modifies direct and indirect identifiers so data cannot be re-identified. Encryption is a process that uses mathematical techniques to convert or transform data into an unreadable format to prevent it from being read except by authorized parties. Synthetic data refers to artificially manufactured data as an alternative to real-world data. There are some other advanced techniques, some of which have only recently become available, or at least feasible in practice, with recent advances in computing power and software techniques. Chapter 7 goes into more detail.

Data Processing Strategy

This must be one of the more substantial sections in your strategy. It may be said that, in principle, we will process and store all data of users locally and only transfer aggregated or anonymized data to our central data hub for analysis. Or it may say all processing of personal data is done in our office in country X, and nothing is stored locally longer than it is needed for a transaction. However, it would not go into details about each data element.

Optimizing data flows

After having taken stock of the countries where your data is located and which data is needed where for processing, a good thing to do would be to make a matrix of these countries in the following way:

	Brazil	Canada	China	EU	India	South Africa	Singapore	US
Brazil				medium				
Canada				easy				
China								
EU	hard	easy	hard		hard	hard	hard	easy
India	easy	easy	easy	easy		easy	easy	easy
South Africa	medium	medium	medium	medium	medium		medium	medium
Singapore				easy				
US	easy	easy	easy	easy	easy	easy	easy	

When developing a strategy of where to keep or move data for processing or further use, this matrix will help you decide how complex each choice will be. For instance, if

EU → India is problematic, but India → EU is not, you might decide to consolidate your data in the EU for processing.

Consent management

Many regulations require obtaining consent from data subjects to store their personal data. And where there is no such regulation, you may well choose to do so to provide transparency and build trust with your customers and partners. This seems easy at first—a simple checkbox on the data entry form explaining how the data will be used (or a link to a privacy policy, which very few people will bother to click).

When looking at the details, however, managing consent is complex and, in some way, almost reflects the entire challenge of multi-national data privacy management on a smaller scale.

Let us look at the example of the e-commerce company we have (virtually) owned throughout this book. We may have obtained consent from a particular customer in a particular country on a particular date for a particular set of purposes. The terms and conditions or our privacy policy may have changed over time, so it is important to know when this consent was obtained. The context is equally important: what did we say we would use the data for? Likely, over time, our business analytics, marketing, customer support, or product teams will come up with new uses for the data, and we need to be able to check those against the original context. To complicate matters further, data subjects have the right to withdraw their consent under many regulations. You can see that managing consent may well require policies, procedures, and a data management tool.

The use of data protection impact assessments

A data protection impact assessment (DPIA) is an evaluation tool to assess privacy risks when processing personal data to minimize risks and ensure compliance with privacy laws and regulations. The DPIA is a requirement under the GDPR at the start of a new project that is likely to involve "a high risk" to other people's personal information.[21] When new changes are introduced by an organization that affects the processing of personal information, it is recommended to conduct a DPIA.

The high-level process when conducting DPIAs involves first the **preparation and preliminary analysis** to determine whether a DPIA is required. Some

---

[21] https://gdpr.eu/data-protection-impact-assessment-template/

organizations have a threshold assessment, sometimes in the form of a questionnaire that checks if personal information is collected, stored, used, or disclosed. When it is determined that a DPIA needs to be conducted, the planning takes place, such as the timeline, risk model to be used, and who will be performing the analysis. The second step involves the **analysis and mapping of information flows**. This is where the process of documenting data flows is conducted. This is where the analysis of what personal information will be collected, used, and disclosed, where it will be stored, how it will be protected, who has access, and why it needs to be handled in a particular way. Once this is done, the **privacy impact analysis and assessment** are conducted. Risks and vulnerabilities are identified, and options are considered and recommended for risk removal, minimization, or mitigation. It will be important to consider compliance with privacy laws and regulations when analyzing risks and choosing recommendations for responding to those risks. All this information needs to be **reported and documented** in a DPIA template. It will also be important to monitor the implementation of the DPIA recommendations.

There are DPIA templates that are made available from different organizations and agencies worldwide. It would be important to note that these templates may vary by jurisdiction depending on the privacy requirements based on different laws and regulations.

Privacy by Design

These well-known principles are best practices in organizations with strong data privacy cultures. In fact, Privacy by Design is a requirement in some regulations, for instance, Brazil's LGPD.

Privacy by Design is a framework initially developed by Dr. Ann Cavoukian, the former privacy commissioner of Ontario, Canada. It is a framework that is based on proactively embedding privacy into the design and operation of IT systems, networked infrastructure, and business practices. It consists of a set of 7 principles as described in the Privacy by Design resource from the Privacy Commissioner of Ontario:[22]

1. **Proactive, not Reactive; Preventative, not Remedial.** Anticipate, identify, and prevent privacy-invasive events before they occur.

2. **Privacy as the Default Setting.** Build the maximum degree of privacy into the default settings for any system or business practice. Doing so will keep a user's privacy intact, even if they choose to do nothing.

3. **Privacy Embedded into Design.** Embed privacy settings into the design and architecture of information technology systems and business

---

[22] https://www.ipc.on.ca/wp-content/uploads/2018/01/pbd-1.pdf

practices instead of implementing them after the fact as an add-on.

4. **Full Functionality — Positive-Sum, not Zero-Sum.** Accommodate all legitimate interests and objectives in a positive-sum manner to create a balance between privacy and security because it is possible to have both.

5. **End-to-End Security — Full Lifecycle Protection.** Embed strong security measures to the complete lifecycle of data to ensure secure management of the information from beginning to end.

6. **Visibility and Transparency — Keep it Open.** Assure stakeholders that privacy standards are open, transparent, and subject to independent verification.

7. **Respect for User Privacy — Keep it User-Centric** Protect the interests of users by offering strong privacy defaults, appropriate notice, and empowering user-friendly options.

The interplay between the data privacy strategy and the data strategy

Earlier in this book, we mentioned the connection between the data privacy strategy and the data strategy of your organization. It is important to understand the link.

One might argue that the data privacy strategy should be part of the data strategy. That is certainly possible. But it isn't just a subset of data strategy—it's a foundational layer. When a company determines how to collect, process, store, and analyze data, it must simultaneously consider how these actions align with privacy regulations, stakeholder expectations, and ethical considerations. The absence of a robust data privacy strategy can jeopardize the broader data initiatives and objectives by exposing the organization to legal, reputational, and operational risks.

Operational synergy

Both strategies, when aligned, can bring about operational synergies. For instance, companies might consolidate their data silos to streamline analytics as part of their data strategy. Here, the data privacy strategy can guide which data is brought together, ensuring that sensitive personal information isn't unnecessarily amalgamated, thereby minimizing risks.

A strong data privacy strategy ensures compliance with regulations and builds trust with customers, partners, and stakeholders. When individuals see that a company is using their data responsibly, in alignment with a well-thought-out strategy, it enhances brand loyalty and customer retention.

Tensions

There might also be areas of tension between data objectives and data privacy. On the one hand, the aim is to make the best use of data to remain competitive. On the other hand, caution is needed to treat data appropriately, not run afoul of laws, and not betray customers' trust. A data strategy often aims at innovative uses of data – predictive analytics, machine learning, and other forms of AI. The data privacy strategy must ensure that such innovations are grounded in responsible data practices. It evaluates the ethical implications, consent requirements, and potential risks of new data uses, ensuring innovations don't overstep boundaries.

Alignment

Ideally, both strategies should be developed in tandem. Privacy experts should sit at the table when the data strategy is being discussed and vice versa. If your organization does not have a formal data strategy yet, you will have an opportunity to do this. However, in many organizations, a data strategy already exists (with some elements of data privacy included). In this case, it would be useful to suggest a review of the data strategy, with the understanding that most of it will stay in place, but with an openness to make some updates where topics touch on data privacy. As we have said, the data privacy strategy cannot be a static document—it will require periodic reviews. The same is true for the data strategy. In these times, where both data and related technologies are evolving so rapidly, it should be obvious that a data strategy should be reviewed at least yearly.

Other strategies and frameworks in your organization

Apart from the data strategy, there may be other strategies and frameworks in your organization that have some overlap with Data Privacy.

Risk management

Some organizations may have an explicit Risk *Management framework*. That will probably speak about data protection and include data breaches that will expose the company's information, including personal information. The legal, operational, and reputational risk of breaches of personal information are areas where the data privacy strategy and the risk management framework overlap and need to be aligned.

Responsible technology

Your organization may also have a policy, strategy, or framework on *Responsible Technology*. A responsible tech framework encompasses ethical considerations when developing and deploying technology. One of the aspects it often emphasizes is the creation or use of technology solutions that prioritize the protection of user data and respect individuals' privacy rights. As such, it would be the development of practices and policies that ensure transparent data collection, secure storage, informed consent, and the ability for users to control their data. Privacy by design may be a recommendation in a responsible tech framework. As such, it can be very helpful to a data privacy strategy and should be fully incorporated.

Alignment with the IT strategy

Implementing a data privacy strategy in an organization depends heavily on the IT infrastructure, policies, and operations. Therefore, it is worth looking at how the IT strategy relates to the data privacy strategy we are developing. The IT strategy outlines the technological road map to support an organization's objectives. This means supporting operations and making the day-to-day work efficient with convenient and dependable infrastructure. But it also means preventing harmful events. Data protection is an important part of IT security objectives. Data misuse, whether intentional or unintentional, needs to be avoided. This is where the data privacy strategy comes in to help reduce those risks.

At the heart of any robust IT strategy is the intent to enhance operations, innovate, and optimize resource allocation. Yet, every technological endeavor often comes with a data footprint. Whether deploying a new cloud solution or adopting an IoT framework, the associated data flow and storage must be evaluated for privacy implications. The data privacy strategy serves as a lens through which IT initiatives can be reviewed to ensure they don't inadvertently compromise data protection standards.

IT security

IT Security is an area where IT and Data Privacy must join forces. A core component of the data privacy strategy is ensuring the security of personal data. This directly correlates with IT strategy's emphasis on cybersecurity. Analysis done in the context of Data Privacy can highlight high-risk data or transactions. Data Privacy policies that prescribe data minimization, encryption, or retention schedules can help reduce risk by minimizing the impact of data breaches when they occur.

When IT and Data Privacy are aligned, organizations can ensure that technological infrastructures support business operations and guarantee that data is encrypted, access is controlled, and potential breaches are swiftly addressed.

Tools and technologies

To effectively implement a data privacy strategy, IT tools are indispensable. We have mentioned data governance tools such as a data catalog and privacy-enhancing tools such as encryption or anonymization. Often, they are not standalone tools that can carry out a particular function, say encrypting a file. Still, they are technologies that need to be integrated with other enterprise tools in the organization to be integrated with workflows. You can see that it is not just a matter of IT providing some tools. The use of these technologies must become part of the IT strategy. Ideally, both strategies should share a unified vision, emphasizing the importance of data protection in all technological pursuits.

Collaboration

A few actions can be taken to help foster an effective collaboration between the IT and Data Privacy teams:

- *Cross-Training*: IT personnel should be trained in data privacy principles, while privacy teams should clearly understand technological frameworks.

- *Shared Platforms*: Adopt platforms that integrate privacy-by-design features. This will ensure that IT implementations naturally embed privacy controls.

- *Continuous Dialogue*: Foster open communication channels between IT and Data Privacy teams. Regular sync-ups can ensure that any technological changes are vetted for privacy implications.

The collaboration between IT and Data Privacy is one of the most important dynamics that can make or break a data privacy strategy.

Developing a strategy for a multinational organization to address data privacy, particularly in the context of cross-border data movements, requires a holistic approach.

By now, you have learned all the elements needed to formulate such a strategy:

- Understand data privacy regulations in each country where the company operates or transfers data.

- Data Flows and Classification—assess the company's data inventory and identify the types of data collected, processed, stored, and transferred across borders. Classify data based on sensitivity, ensuring that highly sensitive data receives heightened protection.

- Manage Risks—assess the data privacy-related risks in your operations and mitigate these risks with policies and measures, such as data minimization and changes in data flows or processing.

- Formulate an approach that is right for your organization, be it principles-based, risk-based, standards-based, or technology-driven.

- Formulate a strategy outline and finally flesh out the full strategy.

You have also understood that creating partnerships with various stakeholders is important while drafting this strategy. You need to have their buy-in because implementation will be impossible without them.

CHAPTER 6

Strategy Implementation

This book is about writing a strategy, which can be a big task that can easily take several months. Implementation of the strategy is a separate task. The implementation is the next effort that will involve many people across the organization. The Data Privacy Officer (DPO) may lead this effort, or someone else with the ability and authority to make the necessary organizational changes. It may well be you as the person who drafted the strategy.

Creating an implementation plan

While the actual implementation is beyond our scope, you may want to include with your strategy a high-level plan for the implementation. This could be included as a section in your strategy, but we recommend keeping it separate. The strategy document will have lasting value as a reference (although it will need to be updated over time). In contrast, the implementation plan describes a one-time effort that will become obsolete once completed.

Like any project plan, the implementation plan will include timeframes, resources (financial investments and human effort), responsibilities, change management, risks, and contingency plans. It would be useful to compartmentalize the plan and its activities into different focus areas, such as people, governance, technology, and company culture. We will discuss these different areas in the following sections.

People

CPO and DPO roles and responsibilities

The Chief Privacy Officer (CPO) is a senior-level executive responsible for overseeing and implementing the privacy program for the organization. Depending on the organization and its size, this appointed officer may have a privacy team to help them with data protection and privacy efforts. In addition, there may also be data protection and privacy focal points assigned in the different departments of the company that liaise with the Chief Privacy Officer.

The Data Protection Officer (DPO) oversees and complies with privacy laws and regulations. GDPR has provided conditions wherein organizations are required to appoint a DPO, who will provide guidance and advice to the organization to comply with GDPR requirements. GDPR specifically assigns six major tasks[23] to the DPO:

- To receive comments and questions from data subjects related to the processing of their personal data and the GDPR.

- To inform an organization and its employees of their obligations under the GDPR and any other applicable EU member state data protection provisions.

- To monitor an organization's compliance with the GDPR and any other applicable EU member state data protection provisions, train staff on compliance, and perform audits.

- To perform data protection impact assessments.

- To cooperate with the data protection supervisory authority.

- To act as the focal point for the data protection supervisory authority on matters relating to processing personal data and other matters, where appropriate.

It is recommended that the DPO should not report to the CPO to ensure independence and impartiality. Therefore,

---

[23] https://gdpr.eu/data-protection-officer/

the DPO should report to top-level management, such as the CEO or the board. The feasibility and practicality of implementing the reporting lines depend on the organization's set-up, size, and needs.

Some organizations will also have a CDO (Chief Data Officer). This role is not specifically related to Data Protection of Privacy but more broadly oversees the data strategy for the organization. Their primary goal is to ensure that data is used to support business outcomes. Of course, they will be aware of the importance (and legal requirements) of handling personal data with care, but usually, personal data will only be a small portion of the data used in an organization. In organizations where both a CDO and CPO or DPO exist, these roles will clearly need to work closely together.

The privacy committee

A privacy committee or council should be created to support data protection and privacy governance matters. The group should comprise major stakeholders such as legal, HR, IT, security, procurement, and others. They may make strategic decisions concerning the implementation of privacy efforts. It is critical to define the roles and responsibilities of the group in general as well as each specific member and to maintain a record of meetings and decisions made by the group.

Major stakeholders

As mentioned above, implementing privacy efforts requires collaboration with different stakeholders such as legal, HR, IT, security, procurement, compliance, and many others. A couple of examples of stakeholders that we would like to highlight are the following: (i) the Human Resources (HR) team handles the personal data of employees. Since employees have privacy rights, HR needs to ensure that the processing of data is subject to the organization's policies and procedures; (ii) the communications team is responsible for internal communications in the company to raise awareness and outreach efforts on data privacy, and for external communications to the consumers and the public to show transparency of the company's data practices. This would also be a good opportunity to present the company's privacy practices as a strategic differentiator by promoting and reinforcing trust in a company's services and products.

Governance

The implementation plan should include activities on the organization's development of governance instruments. This can be looked through the lens of the privacy operational lifecycle[24] that covers the following phases: (i) assess scenarios, gaps, and maturity levels in the privacy program; (ii) protect data throughout its lifecycle by implementing security controls and practices; (iii) sustain the privacy program by monitoring, auditing, and other activities; (iv) respond to data subject requests and incidents.

Based on the above, it would include developing a privacy policy and privacy notices, standard operating processes and procedures regarding receiving and responding to data subject requests, conducting a data impact assessment, managing data breaches, data mapping, and other key activities. It would also be important to include the activity on developing data-sharing agreements and contract clauses, particularly for sharing data across different countries and regions. It would also be important to note that data protection and privacy committees and working groups, as mentioned in the above section, must be established and operational to support governance activities.

Consent management

Consent management can be tricky, especially in a large and international organization where data flows among

---

[24] https://iapp.org/resources/article/privacy-operational-life-cycle-2/

different departments and countries. Consent will have been given in a particular context. Users may have the right to withdraw their consent and request that their data be deleted. This makes consent management one of the key information management objectives in implementing a data privacy strategy and one that needs the right policies, processes, and technology to manage well.

Incident response

Of particular importance are the policies and processes for incident response. When data breaches occur, the organization must respond quickly to contain the problem. The IT team needs to resolve the issue from a technical perspective. Laws or regulations may require data breach notifications to the government or data subjects. A general crisis communications strategy would also be advisable to inform the public in a way that provides reassurance where possible and prevents escalation.

Procurement

Policies and procedures must be developed and remain to ensure privacy compliance when procuring services, technologies, and tools from vendors. It is imperative to perform due diligence checks to ensure vendors' products comply with specific laws and regulations that your organization has to comply with, including on-site audits or reviewing audit reports. When it comes to contracts, there must be clauses to clearly define all parties' responsibilities and obligations, reduce liability, and mitigate non-compliance risks.

Technology

One of the major components of an implementation plan is technology. This refers to platforms and tools to help implement data protection and privacy activities to support the strategy. In this area, feasibility studies and business cases for the need for such tools need to be developed and analyzed. These tools could include an inventory of systems and PII data, a platform to manage the data protection and privacy program (managing data subject requests, performing data classification and labeling, data mapping, etc.), and privacy-enhancing technologies. It would also be important to ensure adequate funding is available to implement such tools.

Company culture

There are a number of initiatives that can help foster a data protection and privacy culture within a company. One of the ways is through employee training and awareness efforts. This can be started in parallel with the implementation. An organization must invest heavily in training and awareness as it provides employees with guidance on what is expected to ensure that their actions align with the company's privacy policy and procedures. Training activities can cater to a wide variety of users— awareness training for all employees, more in-depth training for data protection and privacy focal points, specific technical training for IT staff, and certification training for the data protection and privacy team. Socializing the strategy and providing training are activities that can complement each other well.

Outreach activities such as seminars, brown-bag lunches, or meetings with departments or groups would also complement the training and increase awareness of the importance of data protection and privacy initiatives.

It would also be beneficial to learn from similar organizations and companies their experience creating and implementing the strategy to apply them as lessons learned. Working with other organizations would also open doors to new opportunities and be a good opportunity to develop and strengthen partnerships on data protection and privacy.

CHAPTER 7

Emerging Technologies' Impact on Data Privacy

The world is changing rapidly, especially in terms of digital information. This poses challenges to data privacy and protection because new technologies have new ways of using and disseminating information. For instance, credit card companies may have developed practices of selling data anonymously in the 1990s or 2000s, but they may have been surprised when new data analytics and AI tools and improved computing power made it easy to de-anonymize the data. The drive for companies to be the first to market with certain consumer gadgets often results in data protection taking a back seat. This chapter will look at some of these technologies.

Artificial intelligence

Artificial Intelligence (AI) has recently taken the world by storm. Soon, it will be unthinkable for any organization not to use AI in some form, lest they be left behind.

The fuel that runs AI is data. If you want to monitor patterns for anomalies, predict outcomes, or automate decisions, you need to give the AI access to data, both historical training data and real-time active data.

The various risks of AI systems are well documented— they include bias, discrimination (of individuals or groups), unfairness, and the invasion of privacy, among others. Many of these problems are related to data privacy in some way.

One form of AI, Generative AI, is rapidly being adopted by workers to help write emails, news articles, analytics reports, and even legal arguments. OpenAI's ChatGPT and Google Bard are examples. However, these large AI models have been criticized for using personal data in their training, which they may disclose, bit by bit, in their responses to user queries. Scandals have also been in the news where users put confidential business data such as meeting notes and computer source code into a public platform as part of their query ("prompt"), which caused parts of this data to be shared with other users who asked related questions.

Even when not using public platforms but rather a private AI system within your organization, there is a risk of AI automatically inferring information from personal data it has access to and, therefore, processing it in unexpected ways. As AI likely becomes ubiquitous in organizations in the coming years, it is important that the data privacy strategy recognizes this and mitigates the risks. When AI policies are being formulated, data privacy is one of the more important issues to be addressed.

For instance, the fact that many AI systems are inherently black boxes—even the developers do not know what exactly is going on in the layers of a neural network— brings into question how a Privacy Impact Assessment can be done when the data is used in such an unpredictable AI system.

In Chapter 5, we saw how an important component of designing a data privacy strategy is to analyze how data flows within the organization and where it is processed. In implementing the strategy, you may go into more detail on what *kind* of processing is done on the data. When AI systems (or components within systems) are deployed, it can quickly become unclear what data is being used and how, making compliance with principles, policies, or laws much harder.

The importance of AI in data privacy can be noted when seeing the mention of "automated decisions" (GDPR) or "algorithmic decisions" (c.f. US Algorithmic Accountability Act of 2019[25]) in various legislations. In many cases, the AI systems use personal data and affect

---

[25] See: https://www.congress.gov/bill/116th-congress/house-bill/2231

the data subjects—so they are squarely in the field of interest that a data privacy strategy covers.

If your organization has an AI strategy or policy, that would be extremely relevant for the data privacy strategy. The intimate connection between AI and data privacy requires adjustments in the approach to AI policies and the data privacy mindset.

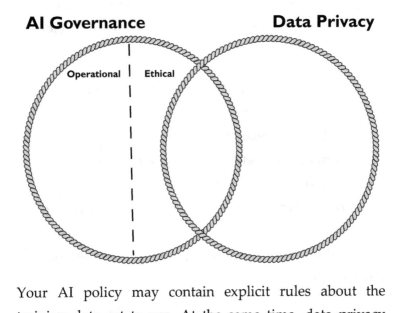

Your AI policy may contain explicit rules about the training data set to use. At the same time, data privacy officers, normally concerned about the data that is held in databases within the company, may be asked to extend their scope to the data used in AI systems. A lot of this data comes from external sources. When it is brought in, it is not typically stored as data in databases but as "knowledge" in neural networks or large language models. However, this data can be reproduced from these models through generative AI applications. So clearly, the organization is holding this data in some form, which may include personal data. As you can see, a whole new way of thinking is required.

Internet of Things (IoT)

The Internet of Things (IoT) is another rapidly growing field with significant data privacy implications. IoT refers to the vast network of interconnected devices, from smart refrigerators and thermostats in homes to complex sensor networks in factories and cities. Many people own at least a few of such devices: a fitness tracker or smartwatch that connects to a central server, a doorbell with a camera that lets you check on visitors or deliveries remotely, a thermostat that can be turned on remotely, or a smoke alarm that can alert you on your phone when something is amiss. Even "smart" appliances such as fridges, ovens, or kettles can be connected to the Internet through Wi-Fi. Life-saving medical devices such as heart or blood pressure monitors are also examples of IoT.

Cars that connect to central servers for anything from diagnostic, crash alters, route planning, or battery management can also be seen as examples of IoT. A 2023 Mozilla Foundation study found that almost all manufacturers' cars have serious flaws and concerns regarding data privacy.

The field of IoT will likely keep growing rapidly in the coming years. However, the convenience and efficiency of these devices come with significant concerns about data privacy and security.

Here are the major data privacy issues with IoT devices:

- **Massive Data Collection**: IoT devices constantly collect data about user behaviors, preferences, and the environment. This data's sheer volume and granularity can give an intimate snapshot of a person's life or a company's operations.

- **Inadequate Data Protection**: Many IoT devices do not have adequate encryption or data protection mechanisms. This makes the data vulnerable to unauthorized access and misuse.

- **Consent**: Often, users are not adequately informed about the type and extent of data their devices are collecting. Consent might be buried in lengthy terms and conditions or not sought at all.

- **Data Sharing**: IoT data might be shared with third parties, including advertisers, without the user's knowledge or consent. This further exposes users to potential privacy risks.

- **Retention**: How long the data is stored and the purpose for which it's retained is often unclear. Indefinite retention poses a risk, especially if there's a data breach.

Here are the major security issues with IoT devices:

- **Vulnerability to Hacking**: Many IoT devices lack robust security features. This makes them easy targets for hackers.

- **Physical Safety**: IoT devices can control physical systems. A compromised device could lead to real-world harm (e.g., tampering with a smart car's braking system or a factory's machinery).

- **Lack of Updates**: Unlike computers or smartphones that receive frequent software updates, many IoT devices may never be updated. This means that even if vulnerabilities are discovered, they might remain unpatched.

These issues are not just theoretical. Security breaches and other unfortunate incidents happen regularly. Just a sampling of high-profile cases in the last few years:

- **Ring Video Doorbell**: In late 2019, reports surfaced that Ring video doorbells had been hacked in multiple incidents, with hackers accessing live feeds and even communicating with homeowners. Ring had been scrutinized for sharing user data with law enforcement agencies without users' explicit consent.

- **Strava Fitness Tracking App**: In 2018, Strava, a fitness tracking app, unintentionally exposed sensitive US military locations via its "heatmap" feature. American soldiers using the app to track their runs inadvertently revealed their paths around military bases.

- **Vizio Smart TVs**: Vizio faced criticism and legal action in 2017 for collecting data on viewers' habits and selling this data to third-party advertisers without the explicit consent of their users.

- **Fisher Price Smart Bear**: This Toy Bear was found to have vulnerabilities in 2015 that could allow hackers to gather personal data about the child and their parents, including names, birthdays, and gender.

- **St. Jude Medical's Implantable Cardiac Devices**: In 2017, the US FDA confirmed vulnerabilities in St. Jude Medical's implantable cardiac devices, which could allow unauthorized access and potentially harm patients.

- **iKettle**: This smart kettle was found to have security vulnerabilities that allowed hackers to access home Wi-Fi passwords through the kettle.

Of course, if your company produces or sells a smart device that collects and/or transmits data, you should definitely review this together with technical experts from a data privacy and data protection perspective. But even if your organization uses any IoT devices, it is worthwhile to check what type of data is being sent through the devices and, if any, contains personal data. The data collection may not be obvious. For example, if your trucks deliver goods to customers, and they are equipped with tracking devices to be able to efficiently plan routing, these trackers will have the customers' addresses.

Privacy Enhancing Technologies (PETs)

In Chapter 5, we have already discussed some technologies that are commonly used today to support data privacy, such as anonymization (or pseudonymization) and encryption. A good number of new, advanced techniques are also coming onto the horizon.

Recent years have seen rapid progress in a number of technologies that are of great use to data privacy. Some of these techniques have been explored in academic literature for much longer but remained theoretical possibilities that were not feasible in practice. However, many of these are now becoming practical tools with advances in computing power and software techniques. It is not only the increased computing power that contributed to the progress in PETs. There is also an increase in interest from the tech community, which has acknowledged the importance of data privacy in today's world.

Homomorphic encryption

Homomorphic Encryption (HE) is a method of encryption that allows for computations to be carried out on the encrypted data without needing decryption first. This can be useful for privacy-preserving computations in the cloud.

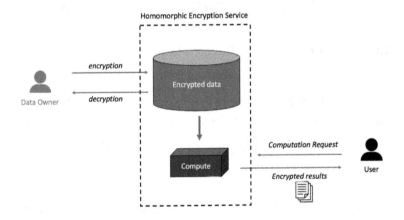

There are different levels to HE:

- *Partially Homomorphic Encryption (PHE)* supports only one type of operation, either addition or multiplication, but not both.

- *Somewhat Homomorphic Encryption (SHE)* supports addition and multiplication but only for a limited number of times. After a certain number of operations, the noise added during each encryption operation accumulates, making the decryption of the resulting ciphertext error-prone or impossible.

- *Fully Homomorphic Encryption (FHE)* supports both addition and multiplication operations an unlimited number of times without causing decryption errors. This is the most powerful form of homomorphic encryption and has been a major topic of cryptographic research.

FHE has been described as the holy grail of cloud security. It will definitely be an extremely useful solution for IoT design. However, it has been hard to implement due to being computationally very intensive and complicated to use, which means it hasn't been a realistic option in the past. But that may be changing. With faster processors and better software, such as the excellent open-source openFHE library,[26] it is now getting closer to becoming a practical solution.

---

[26] See: https://www.openfhe.org/

Statistical disclosure control

Statistical disclosure control refers to the application of measures to protect the identity of a person or organization from being identified in the data in surveys and research studies. It applies de-identification methods such as removing direct personal identifiers and applying generalization or suppression rules on quasi-identifiers. These fields do not directly identify a person but, when combined with other fields, can help identify an individual. There are techniques developed to reduce the risk of anonymity using suppression and generalization methods:

- **K-anonymity:**[27] refers to a technique wherein the resulting dataset has at least "k" records that are indistinguishable from each other concerning certain "identifying" attributes

- **L-diversity:**[28] refers to a technique that takes the k-anonymity method and the resulting dataset has at

---

27 Samarati, P.; Sweeney, L. Protecting Privacy when Disclosing Information: k-Anonymity and Its Enforcement through Generalization and Suppression. https://dataprivacylab.org/dataprivacy/projects/kanonymity/paper3.pd f

[28] Machanavajjhala, A, Et. Al. (2007) L-Diversity: Privacy Beyond K-Anonymity

least "l" distinct values in each group of k records for sensitive attributes.

- **T-closeness:**[29] refers to a technique that takes the l-diversity method further by reducing the granularity of data.

An open-source data anonymization tool that provides the above capabilities plus other data privacy methods is the ARX Data Anonymization tool.[30] Many publications, most of them in the medical and healthcare field, have used the ARX tool.

Differential privacy

Differential privacy is a framework that adds controlled noise to datasets to protect individual data points. While relatively new, it is already fully in use by many organizations—it has been adopted by major tech entities like Apple and Google for user data analytics. The US Census Bureau uses differential privacy to be able to share data with the public without running the risk that data elements might be traced back to specific individuals.

---

[29] Li, N., et al (2007). "T-Closeness: Privacy Beyond k-Anonymity and l-Diversity

[30] See https://arx.deidentifier.org/

A great open-source framework developed by people at Harvard University is OpenDP.[31] The ARX data anonymization tool mentioned in the previous section also provides differential privacy capabilities.

Zero-knowledge proofs

Zero-knowledge Proofs (ZKPs) are cryptographic methods that allow one party to prove to another that a statement is true without revealing any information about the statement itself.

These have found applications in blockchain and other domains, emphasizing the broadening landscape of privacy-conscious technologies. In particular, the zk-SNARKs and zk-STARKs protocols are popular examples. Zcash, a cryptocurrency, utilizes ZKPs for transaction privacy.

Multi-party computation

Multi-party Computation (MPC) is a cryptography subfield that enables multiple parties to collaboratively compute a function over their inputs while keeping those inputs private.

---

[31] See: https://opendp.org/

Imagine various participants, each with a piece of secret information, working together to obtain a common result without revealing their individual secrets. For example, a classic example of MPC is the "millionaires' problem," where two millionaires want to determine who is wealthier without revealing their actual net worth to each other. Using MPC, they can do this.

MPC's potential real-world applications are vast. For instance, in medical research, institutions could aggregate health data to detect patterns or analyze the efficacy of treatments without accessing individual patient records, thereby preserving privacy. Similarly, businesses can utilize MPC for secure data mining and analytics, gleaning insights from combined datasets without exposing proprietary or sensitive data.

Federated learning

Federated Learning (FL) is a machine learning approach that addresses data privacy and security concerns. Instead of centralizing data, FL trains models directly at the source on users' devices, such as smartphones or tablets. Once models are locally trained, only model updates or gradients (rather than raw data) are sent to a central server for aggregation. This ensures that sensitive data never leaves the user's device.

This reduces the risk of data breaches, as personal data doesn't need to be transferred across networks. It can also be an effective tool to leverage data for analysis while complying with data transfer rules in regulations like GDPR. However, FL isn't trivial. It requires algorithms that can handle asynchronous updates from various sources. An uneven data distribution across devices can also lead to biased models if not addressed correctly. However, FL holds much promise. Enabling model training without compromising user privacy allows business interests to leverage data while adhering to privacy principles or laws.

Synthetic data

Synthetic data refers to artificially manufactured data as an alternative to real-world data. The objective of using synthetic data is to facilitate the sharing of data and the development of algorithms between different organizations and entities without compromising privacy. The synthetic data retains the original data structure and properties, which can be used to train and test machine learning models or test applications.

The Synthetic Data Vault[32] is an open-source tool developed by the Massachusetts Institute of Technology

---

[32] https://news.mit.edu/2020/real-promise-synthetic-data-1016

(MIT) researchers Kalyan Veeramachaneni and his collaborators for creating and using synthetic data sets.

Decentralized identity systems

Decentralized Identity Systems (DIS) utilize blockchain (or other decentralized architectures) to give users control over their own identity information.

Traditional centralized identity systems, controlled by singular entities, have often been targets for data breaches, risking the privacy and security of individual users. In contrast, decentralized systems distribute control across a network, lessening single points of vulnerability.

At the core of these systems is the concept of "self-sovereign identity." This means users create and manage their online identity—they have complete control over their identity data, deciding who accesses it, when, and for what purpose. In DIS, the personal data is not stored in centralized databases but in decentralized systems such as distributed ledgers or blockchains.

From a data privacy standpoint, this is transformative. Allowing individuals to share only verifiable claims or proofs instead of raw data minimizes unnecessary data exposure. For example, to prove one's age, one might only need to demonstrate that they're over 18 without revealing the exact birthdate.

There are still challenges, such as interoperability of these systems or widespread adoption. However, the promise of a framework where data privacy is intrinsic and not added-on is an exciting prospect from a data privacy point of view. Decentralized identities are an essential component of the vision of Web3 applications and hold many other benefits, so there are good reasons why they may take off shortly.

Secure environments

What if the technology environment you store and process your data in was built up from the ground to be secure? This will provide many new opportunities for data protection.

Secure operating systems

You can take things to another level of security by running applications in an operating system that has security built in by design. Qubes OS[33] is a free, open-source, security-oriented operating system for single-user desktop computing. It's run on a virtual machine.

---

[33] See: https://www.qubes-os.org

SELinux (Security Enhanced Linux)[34] is a well-known security-related extension to Linux that contains many modern concepts and tools. SELinux came out of research by the US National Security Agency. It focuses on role-based and mandatory access controls, following the principle of least privilege. It is free and open source.

Tails OS[35] is another example, which is more geared towards protecting against

surveillance and censorship but may have applications for data privacy.

Currently, these tools are for single users and probably not relevant for the design of a corporate data privacy strategy. But they are interesting nevertheless, and maybe these concepts will be scaled up at some point in the future so that entire data centers can be run in an inherently secure environment.

Secure hardware enclaves

What if we took security by design even further down, to the level of the processor (CPU)? That is actually being done already—they are called Secure Hardware Enclaves,

---

[34] See: https://github.com/SELinuxProject/selinux

[35] See: https://tails.net/

and examples are Intel's Software Guard Extensions (SGX) and ARM's TrustZone.

These enclaves create isolated, protected zones within processors where data can be processed without exposure to the rest of the system, even if other parts are compromised. From a data privacy perspective, this offers an extremely advanced level of protection. Secure enclaves can protect sensitive data from both software-based and even certain hardware-based attacks. When a system may be compromised by malware, the enclave provides a safe haven where data remains encrypted and inaccessible.

The technology is not widely used yet, but it may become more common in the future. It is particularly significant for cloud computing environments, where multiple clients share resources. Using enclaves, data can be processed securely without the cloud provider or other clients having the capability to view or tamper with it.

Mix networks

Another vulnerable aspect of the digital environment is the networks between servers. Mix Networks (or "Mixnets") try to solve that using a cryptographic technique to improve user anonymity and data privacy in digital communications.

Mixnets work by routing users' messages through a series of nodes (known as mixes) in a non-linear order. Each mix shuffles the order of messages and employs cryptographic techniques to alter their appearance. When messages exit the network, their path becomes nearly impossible to trace back to their origin, preserving the sender's anonymity.

Unlike traditional encryption methods, which focus on content privacy, Mixnets focus on metadata privacy. While encrypted messages can't easily be read, they can still be tracked based on metadata (like the sender, recipient, or timestamp). By randomizing and obscuring this metadata, Mixnets protect the "who," "when," and "to whom" of communication, not just the "what."

As with other technologies discussed in this chapter, Mixnets are a technical possibility without broad adoption yet. The overhead of running Mixnets and the lack of standardization are hurdles. But as data privacy and protection are increasingly recognized as important and often mandatory, this technology, too, may start to see wider implementation.

The Metaverse

In 2020, everyone was talking about the Metaverse. By 2023, the term was decidedly out of fashion. Even Facebook, which was so bullish that they had changed their name to Meta, got rather quiet on the Metaverse and focused on AI. But Virtual Reality (VR) and Augmented Reality (AR) are still there—new advances are being announced regularly in hardware (headsets) and software (virtual worlds). The idea of a Metaverse may well come back at some point.

"The Metaverse" is still only a concept. Elements of it exist in the form of online virtual games, business applications that allow VR meetings using headsets, and more. But the idea of an integrated experience that forms a parallel virtual world is a vision of the future that has not happened yet.

For this book, let us define the Metaverse informally as a *virtual environment* or a collection of interoperable virtual worlds. These virtual worlds can be experienced in various ways, especially through VR/AR *headsets*. Companies like Meta/Oculus, HTC, Sony, Samsung, and Magic Leap have released headsets, and new players are constantly entering the market. The Metaverse is *persistent*—that is, unlike a computer game that might reset itself for a new session, the virtual worlds continue to exist. The Metaverse is massively *multi-user*: thousands or millions of users are present (in the form of avatars or other representations) in the virtual world at the same time, and they interact. That interaction makes the world "alive". It allows for communication (conversations, parties, or seminars), collaboration (business meetings, joined efforts, or quests), competition (e.g., in virtual games), and commerce (selling virtual goods, sometimes with real-life aspects as well, such a concert tickets or fashion accessories).

Many modern VR/AR headsets have sensors that monitor the slightest head movements and even eye tracking through small cameras in the headset that are pointed inwards at the eyes of the user. This way, the headset and, thereby, the provider of the Metaverse experience, have unprecedented access to the behavior and emotions of its users. In the past, an advertiser would know if you clicked on their website advertisement. In the Metaverse, they will know whether you glanced at it for a fraction of a second or paused to look at it for multiple seconds and if it triggered any emotional reaction. In addition, every movement you make in these virtual worlds, every action, every pause, every communication you have with other inhabitants of the world, is registered—they have to be because the platform needs to generate your virtual experience in real time, depending on your activity.

From a data privacy perspective, the behavioral and biometric information collected in the Metaverse, or in any virtual environment for gaming, social interaction, or business, clearly takes things to a new level. The fact that in these virtual worlds, the physical location and nationality of the users behind the avatars that interact are not necessarily known, makes the applicability of data privacy laws even harder. If the Metaverse someday becomes a significant part of the way we experience life (and with AR, the lines between real and virtual lives may start to blur!) and all of that life gets monitored constantly, a new set of data ethics, principles, and laws will be needed.

The technologies that enable the Metaverse—virtual 3D environments, transaction processing, and VR/AR hardware are all continuing to evolve. In addition, the recent advances in Generative AI mean it is no longer necessary to create 3D models of objects and landscapes in virtual worlds by hand (a time-consuming process) as they can be automatically generated in high resolution and unlimited quantities. As the technological challenges are being resolved, The Metaverse, in whatever form, may come into being at some point. If that happens, data privacy will be an important issue. If your organization plans to have a presence in the Metaverse at some point, this should be addressed in the data privacy strategy.

Conclusion

Congratulations on finishing this book! We have covered a lot in the past seven chapters.

We've come to understand that data privacy isn't a monolithic concept. It differs significantly from one country to another, influenced by cultural values, historical experiences, and socio-political dynamics. Some nations prioritize individual rights and personal freedoms, while others weigh the benefits of data to the economy more heavily.

Moreover, public trust is fragile these days, and businesses should recognize that data privacy is more than just compliance – it's about building trust and demonstrating respect for the individuals behind the data. A breach or (intentional or accidental) misuse of personal data poses legal and financial risks and harms a company's reputation.

Formulating a robust data privacy strategy demands understanding the global environment and local nuances. It also requires a thorough understanding of the organization's data flows and use. This requires a dedicated team, comprehensive training, and a commitment to data privacy principles.

As the world becomes increasingly digital, the personal data of billions of people are constantly being created, transferred, and stored across multiple countries and systems. Data privacy will continue to evolve as new uses of data arise.

Rather than seeing data privacy as a necessary evil, one could see it as an opportunity. It is an opportunity for organizations to distinguish themselves through integrity and trust.

We hope you enjoyed reading this book and that it helps strengthen your organization's approach to data privacy.

Resources

If you would like to go deeper into some data privacy-related topics, here are books, articles, and online trainings that we recommend for further study.

Data privacy in general

- "Privacy Program Management: Tools for Managing Privacy Within Your Organization" by Russell Densmore, et. al. This is an IAPP publication that is used for the Certified Information Privacy Manager program and provides information on managing privacy program governance and operations.

- "An Introduction to Privacy for Technology Professionals" by Travis D. Breaux, et. al. This is an IAPP publication that is used for the Certified Information Privacy Technologist (CIPT) program and provides information on how privacy and technology intersect and examines critical areas of concern in the industry.

- "Information Privacy Engineering and Privacy by Design" by William Stallings gives an overview of privacy engineering and requirements for compliance with regulations (ISBN: 0135302153)

- IAPP Certification Programs There are three programs: CIPM, CIPT and CIPP. These are thorough, instructor-led trainings (about 12 hours each).

- "Privacy and Standardisation" specialization on Coursera.

This is a set of intermediate-level courses that address data privacy, standardization, and technology topics. Having some familiarity with technology and law is useful before starting this course. It can be audited for free, or payment will get you a certificate. See: https://www.coursera.org/specializations/privacy.

Global data privacy regulations

- "Understanding the GDPR" by the University of Groningen

This is a course on the Future Learn platform that gives an excellent understanding of the GDPR. It takes four weeks to complete (three hours per week of lectures, plus some more self-study perhaps). It is free, or if you like, you can pay a modest fee to obtain a certificate. See:

https://www.futurelearn.com/courses/general-data-protection-regulation

- "Understanding LGPD: basic elements"

This is an introduction to Brazil's Data Privacy regulation from the resources center of IAPP. See: https://iapp.org/resources/article/understanding-the-lgpd-basic-elements/.

Data management

- "DAMA International's Guide to the Data Management Body of Knowledge"

DAMA DMBOK is an authoritative reference book on data management written by leading thinkers in the field. See https://technicspub.com/dmbok2/.

Data privacy-related technologies

- "Practical Data Privacy" by Katharine Jarmul (ISBN: 9781098129460) addresses various PETs from a practical (engineering) perspective.

- "IAPP Privacy Tech Vendor Report." The IAPP releases an annual report on the growth and trends of the privacy technology marketplace. See:

https://iapp.org/resources/article/privacy-tech-vendor-report/

- "UN Guide on Privacy Enhancing-Technologies on Official Statistics." This gives an overview of various PETs. It can be downloaded for free at: https://unstats.un.org/bigdata/task-teams/privacy/guide/2023_UN%20PET%20Guide.pdf

- "Emerging Privacy Enhancing Technologies Current Regulatory and Policy Approaches". This OECD report examines privacy-enhancing technologies and outlines regulatory and policy approaches with regard to these technologies. See: Emerging privacy-enhancing technologies: Current regulatory and policy approaches | OECD Digital Economy Papers | OECD iLibrary (oecd-ilibrary.org)

- "National Strategy to Advance Privacy-Preserving Data Sharing and Analytics" is not meant as a textbook (it is a national strategy), but it has a useful comparison of PETs. See: https://www.whitehouse.gov/wp-content/uploads/2023/03/National-Strategy-to-Advance-Privacy-Preserving-Data-Sharing-and-Analytics.pdf

Index

www.ingramcontent.com/pod-product-compliance
Lightning Source LLC
Chambersburg PA
CBHW071243050326
40690CB00011B/2237